MW01075671

# Find the Primordial Light in You

## GOD Extends His Helping Hand

**Gabriele Publishing House**
P.O. Box 2221, Deering, NH 03244
(844) 576-0937
WhatsApp/Messenger: +49 151 1883 8742
www.Gabriele-Publishing-House.com

*Gabriele*

# Find the
# PRIMORDIAL LIGHT
## in You

## GOD Extends His Helping Hand

THE WORD
THE UNIVERSAL SPIRIT

First Edition, 2010
Published by:
© Universal Life
The Inner Religion
P.O. Box 3549
Woodbridge, CT 06525
U S A

Licensed edition
translated from the original German title:
"Finde zum UR-LICHT in Dir
Die Handreichung GOTTES"
Order No. S 142en

From the Universal Life Series
with the consent of
© Verlag DAS WORT GmbH
im Universellen Leben
Max-Braun-Str. 2
97828 Marktheidenfeld/Altfeld, Germany

The German edition is the work of reference for all
questions regarding the meaning of the contents

All rights reserved

ISBN 978-1-890841-08-9

# Table of Contents

# Foreword

Despite the wars and natural disasters that threaten this world, the light of the divine love streams onto the earth more and more, into this world and to those people who are of goodwill. Whoever is able to watch and analyze the disasters of this world realizes that we human beings are facing a mighty turn of time. The call of the Christ of God resounds again and again: May the one save himself who wants to let himself be saved, before this world passes away!

God, our eternal Father, extends His mighty helping hand through Gabriele, His prophetess and messenger, offering a path of schooling on which we can quickly expand our consciousness, and grow closer to God in us. Ever more people are sensing that the anchor in this difficult time is solely Christ, the bringer of light in the very basis of the soul of every person.

For the first time in written form, this book reflects the contents of a radio program series that was broadcast worldwide. These are also available on CD.

*I Am the Order*
*in God's*
*All-Order.*

Order 1

# Order 1

 hoever watches our world with alert senses asks the question: Can this world be compared to a sinking ship, whose captain has lost his hold on the helm? The crew, the people, are at the mercy of the storms of the high seas, the disasters, wars, terrorism and murder. No person knows anymore in which direction the ship-world is actually drifting.

Many feel they have no hold and have been delivered into the hands of a power that cannot be so easily fathomed. Unfortunately, it has gone so far that almost every person blames the other. The politicians blame the people; they fleece the people financially more and more and the people blame the politicians, the power-hungry who strive only to insure their sinecure and keep their position, not to mention the corruption that has almost become a privilege for those who have money and property.

The chaos of the world, that is turning ever more into a world disaster that escalates from day to day – for the disasters are multiplying, hardship, illness, in-firmity and murder have become the topic of the day. The brutalization of mankind is gaining the upper hand. Everyone is his own best friend, which means that the one fights against the other, be it in thoughts, with words or even in his actions.

When the leaders of the churches are asked where the disasters in this world come from, under which so many people are suffering and why God does not inter-vene, a long rhetorical flood of words is given about the whys and wherefores, more or less a hairsplitting theological answer, that God does not allow one to see into His mysteries – which, in the final analysis means that He is to blame for the spectacle taking place in the world since He does not intervene and that, out of sheer mystery mongering, He, God, lets the people suffer and the earth be violated.

Ever more people are asking about God. They ask if there is a God, at all, and if yes, then why He allows such chaos in the world. A good, experienced analyst, who takes a scrutinizing look at this world, comes to understand that it is not God who is the unfathomable, the "sorcerer," instead, the people are the sorcerer's apprentice, who are satisfied with the theological hair-splitting over the so-called mysteries of God.

Common sense recognizes that this world chaos does not come from God, but that all the generations of mankind have caused it, and that every person has more or less contributed to this disaster. If God, the Eternal, were to bring the planet Earth and everything that romps and plays itself out on it into His divine Order through His word of omnipotence, then tomorrow there would again be this same spectacle of human ignorance that directs itself against the eternal law of God, which is love, unity and freedom. Why? Because the effects and repercussions of human thinking in terms of self-interest – the egotistical, the hunger for power, the domineering tendencies, the greed for profit, the intolerance, arrogance, disparagement, indifference, cold-heartedness and so on – would soon make an appearance again on a small as well as a large scale. In the end, nothing would be better.

As long as the human being does not learn to respect his fellowman, as well as nature and the animal kingdoms, he remains hostile and cruel toward life. He destroys, annihilates and kills whatever stands in his way, and does all this for his own sake.

Because God is love, and because God's love wants to lead His children back into the Father's house through Christ, the loving, eternal Father now extends His helping hand to us again, to lead His willing human children as quickly as possible to His fatherly heart, that beats for every person and for every soul, so that they may draw closer to Him, the Eternal; so that they may learn and experience that He is present in the soul of every human being. He, the great Spirit, wants to give each one of us security and a sense of secureness.

In many facets, Christ and our spiritual teacher, the cherub of divine Wisdom, called Brother Emanuel for us people, have taught us the eternal law that leads to the true life, that makes us independent, free and happy.

Through His instrument, the Eternal reveals that the language of human beings works against the eternal cosmic law. It is all too much interspersed with "ifs" and "buts," with "I want" or "I can't," so that through this, the primordial power of the soul, the core of being, the law of love and kindness, can hardly be addressed.

Our human language is a doubting, confining language, through which a human being cannot make any claims of absoluteness for itself, which causes the person to follow a long way filled with hurdles and tribulations, until he draws closer to his divine heritage, the law of God in his soul.

When we look at this world, many a one says: Time is speeding up and the hours fly by ever more quickly, so that it is high time to look more closely at the instructions of life and to turn back. So many a one feels the urging, the request that comes from deep in his soul, saying: O human being, do not tarry! It is truly high time!

As mentioned, our language separates us from God. This is why the offer of the Eternal follows to address our divine heritage and to do this with the divine absoluteness, which does not know any "ifs" and "buts."

To give an idea of what it means when we human beings affirm and address the absoluteness in us, I still want to take a few words for this.

The law of God consists of the seven basic forces. They are Order, Will, Wisdom and Earnestness, Patience – the same as kindness – Love, Mercy – the same as gentleness. These seven basic forces pulsate in the very basis of our soul.

The earnest person, who wants to grow closer to God in the very basis of his soul, can address the law of God with the full power of the primordial power, for example:

*In the divine cosmic law,*
*in my divine heritage,*
*I am the absolute Order.*

13

Many a one will now say: "But I am not yet orderly. My thoughts and a lot of what I move around and call my property, be it the smallest thing in daily life, aren't yet in order. How can I say: 'In the divine cosmic law, in my divine heritage, I am the absolute Order.'"

To this, the following explanation: The one who makes great effort to put order into his thoughts, into everything that is a part of him as a human being, sets into motion a cosmic seismograph with the certain and decisive statement: "In the divine cosmic law, in my divine heritage, I am the absolute Order." This cosmic seismograph shows him what is not in order. With the power of the absolute Order of the law, which the willing person speaks into the core of being of his soul, he releases negative energy formations in himself – he brings significant aspects of his all-too-human inputs into movement, which are stored as inputs in the particle structure of his soul and in his body. With this, he loosens at the same time unlawful inputs in certain planets, which, via the corresponding planetary constellation, the person who, for example, applies the Absolute Law of Order, becomes aware of.

It is important to know that on this clear-cut path of law, small misdemeanors, which are not relevant in the earthly life and which have harmed no other person, are dissolved, that is, transformed into positive energy, through which the soul increases in light and power. This would be for every person a great chance to find his way into his inner being more rapidly, to his divine origin, his true self; for only God, in the origin of our soul, is the mooring and the secure harbor in this time filled with danger.

The one who earnestly and conscientiously follows this path of the law will very soon become aware of his true origin. His life on earth will totally change before long. He becomes more sensitive, his five senses more clear, his consciousness expands and he gains access to the innermost recesses of his neighbor, to God in his neighbor, just as to all the forces of nature and to the living beings among the animals. He becomes ever more cosmic, that is, all-encompassing and selfless, in his thinking, speaking and doing. His existence on earth is transformed, because he senses and recognizes in many details that God is always present.

The Eternal has directed His instrument to instruct willing people in all seven basic forces in the Absolute Law, to show how it can be applied – of course, only for those who want this, for God is freedom.

According to the will of God, I begin with the divine Order of the law.

Let us be aware that everything is energy, and everything, but everything, radiates. Because the eternal principles of the law are in everything and in all things, each thing, every life form, every person, every being, is a part of the total volume of divine law that is unending. Thus, everything has its place in the unity, in the all-cosmic Being.

According to the spiritual radiation of all material things and forms, each one fits into the divine law respectively, into the wholeness of the law, that consists of the seven basic rays. We call the holistic Being the law of unity.

Let us be aware that everything that surrounds us is radiation. According to its radiation, each thing has its place – either in the law of Order or in the law of Will or in the further principles of the law like Wisdom, Earnestness, Patience – the same as kindness – Love, Mercy – the same as gentleness.

I repeat: Every divine intensity of radiation, together with all other energetic radiations, forms one unity. The material forms envelop, that is, they encompass, the divine law-energies, which, like all things, are also radiation. Material objects and forms – regardless of kind – radiate what we think toward them and with which frame of mind we touch them. So, energies of other people cling to objects, for example, thought energies of people who have worked on the products, wares and the like. The energetic content of every thought – perhaps problematic things, envy, resentment, reproach – can emit to us and influence us, if we have a similar characteristic. That is the unlawful radiation that we can describe as disorder because it moves, not in the Absolute Law of God, but in the law of sowing and reaping.

Every disorder – no matter how slight – is a dissonance, which can influence us, our disposition, our world of thoughts, even our whole behavior. Dissonances of every type also have an effect in and on our body. Depending on the dissonance, we act, for example, in a hectic manner, aggressively, brutally, even to the point of being destructive both to ourselves and to others.

We know that like attracts like. And so, radiation dissonances can make us sick and bring suffering; they can trigger terrorism, crime and wars. Global energetic causal dissonances, that is, causes, which many people or even groups of people have created, can have an effect on the earth and bring about disasters and famine. The effects hit the corresponding people according to their part in this cause, regardless of what nation they belong to at the time.

Every soul in a human being has in its very basis the Absolute Law, the divine heritage of the divine being that we are in the eternal Being. And so, as complete and perfect beings, we are the Absolute Law, which consists of the previously mentioned seven basic forces or powers.

As mentioned, our language puts everything in question, even the Absolute Law, the cosmic law, which is our true, eternal life. Each one of us, who puts something into words, who expresses himself in words, puts himself and others in question. This is the causal language, which separates and divides us from others, and above all, from God, from our true being.

If we want to approach our true being, the Absolute Law of love and unity, then we have to learn – each one of us – to change our way of thinking, by beginning with the first basic power of Order and by first becoming aware of the fact that in the eternal Being, we are the Order in the eternal law of God's Order.

Let us become aware that if we want to truly work with the Absolute Law, if we want to apply it step by step in our daily life, then ever more often during the day, we have to address the Absolute Law in the very basis of our soul – regardless of situation, occurrence or with what objects or things we are occupied – as, for example, "I am the absolute Order in the divine cosmic law, in my divine heritage."

Whoever makes this formulation his own, which in brief form can be, "I am the Order in God's All-Order," sets a seismograph into motion in himself, that calls his attention to where the disorder is in him. The one who sets out to get rid of the disorder and to no longer think and do the same or like things, or the one who sets about putting order in things and objects in his surroundings – depending on what the seismograph signals to him – very gradually approaches the cosmic Order of the law.

The one who decides for this lawful path that leads to the primordial power in the very basis of the soul, that is to say, the one who endorses this not easy, but quick, pathway, makes himself aware at this point that he is addressing the primordial power in his soul and, at the same time, his divine heritage, that is the All-law of love and unity.

Whoever exposes himself to his "seismograph," which brings a lot of disorder into the light of day, now sends impulses with me into the basis of the soul, into the primordial power.

We begin with the power of Order.

Everything is energy! We send the impulse into the core of being of the soul, into the primordial power:

*I am the Order
in God's All-Order.*

*I am the Order
in God's All-Order.*

*I am the Order
in God's All-Order.*

With these impulses of the law we set our seismograph into motion, which will now or in the course of the evening, or even on the next day, show us where there are energetic dissonances that need to be cleared up.

What is important is that we pay attention to these indications and follow them. So we should clear up these dissonances and no longer do the wrongdoing we have recognized.

With this not so easy, but quick, path of the law we begin, plainly and simply, from without to within.

Now, let us come to our daily life. Whether we are in the kitchen, at work, on the street, in the car or anywhere else – over and over again, we should think or speak the impulse into the very basis of our soul:

*I am the Order
in God's All-Order.*

## *I* am the Order
## in God's All-Order.

In time, our senses, too, will begin to react. The disorder – for example, in our home, in the maintenance of our home or apartment, at work, in thoughtless and uncontrolled conversations and much more – jumps into our face, so to speak. Our senses react. Everywhere there is disorder, where there is a lack of purity and cleanliness, where the un-good spreads out, the seismograph begins to act. It does not spare our closets and drawers. Even our body posture, how we walk, what we speak, how we think, what we eat or drink is registered by our seismograph and reflected back to us. At the same time, we realize what we have to get rid of.

As already mentioned, at first, it is all about external things, like, for example, does our clothing fit with our body radiation? Are our shoes in order? Does everything have its order at home, at work? Are the objects in our home in their place?

The more often we become aware that everything is energy and wants to fit itself into the great totality as a radiation intensity, the more we will be stimulated to do what is necessary to bring it into order. If we are aware of this because we have gained experience in it, we will feel on our own body and sense in our own disposition how beneficial it is to put order into the external aspects of our life, to comply with the energetic unity. Soon we will feel better and refreshed, happy, free and united from within.

Then, we will soon be able to grasp our thoughts more clearly and to more clearly perceive our body radiation. We will not only become more sensitive toward our own behavior, but also toward our fellow-man. In ever finer subtleties, we can better grasp our second neighbors: the animals, as well as the world of the plants and minerals – all of nature.

Everything, but everything, wants to have its place in the great totality, be it even the smallest or most inconspicuous thing. Everything is radiation. Every radiation contains the primordial core of divine lawfulness, that strives, yes, urges, ever more toward unity.

Dear brothers, dear sisters, this was only a very small insight into the mighty divine law of All-Radiation that is love and unity.

The one who wants to will join in this great forward thrust with the step that leads into the primordial power, and toward God.

And so, the motto is: May the one who wants to save himself, save himself.

The more often we apply the Order of the law, the more often we put order into our surroundings, into ourselves, the happier and freer we will be.

Dear brothers and sisters, until next time, I wish you all that is good.

A lot, a lot of inner happiness brings a lot, a lot of life!

*Gabi*

*I Am*
*the Order*
*in God's All-Order,*
*which Illuminates*
*My Disposition.*

Order 2

# Order 2

$\mathcal{D}$ear brothers, dear sisters in Christ, the gift of grace of the Eternal One to His willing God-conscious children, to His sons and daughters, which is going out into the whole world, is becoming more and more manifest.

In accordance with the will of God, I begin with a short repetition, so that together we can become aware of His love.

Every soul in a human being has in its very basis the Absolute Law, the divine heritage of the divine being that each of us is in the eternal Being. And so, as complete and perfect beings, we are the Absolute Law, which consists of the seven basic forces of God.

As mentioned, our human language, with its "ifs" and "buts," places everything in question, even the Absolute Law, the cosmic law, which is our true, eternal life. Each one of us, who puts something into words, who expresses himself in words, places himself and others in question. This is the causal language, which separates and divides us from others, and above all, from God, from our true being.

If we want to draw closer to our true being, the Absolute Law of love and unity, then we have to learn – each one of us – to change our way of thinking by beginning with the first basic power of Order and first become aware of the fact that in the eternal Being, we are the Order in the eternal law of God's Order.

Let us be aware that if we want to truly work with the Absolute Law, if we want to apply it step by step in our daily life, then ever more often during the day, we have to address the Absolute Law in the very basis of our soul – regardless of situation, occurrence or with what objects or things we are occupied – as, for example, "I am the absolute Order in the divine cosmic law, in my divine heritage."

If a person makes this formulation his own, which in brief form can be "I am the Order in God's All-Order," and if he applies this sentence, this statement, by letting it become effective in himself and through himself, then he sets into motion in himself a "seismograph" that calls his attention to where there is disorder in him. If a person sets out to discard the disorder and to no longer think and do like or similar things, or if he starts putting order in things and objects in his surroundings – depending on what the seismograph signals to him – then he very gradually draws closer to the cosmic Order of the law.

The one who decides for this lawful path that leads to the primordial power in the very basis of the soul, that is to say, the one who affirms this not easy but quick pathway and wants to take it, makes himself aware at this point that he is addressing the primordial power in his soul and, at the same time, his divine heritage in the innermost part of his soul, which is the All-law of love and unity.

Whoever exposes himself to his "seismograph," which brings a lot of disorder into the light of day, now sends impulses with me into the basis of the soul, into the primordial power.

We begin with the power of Order.

Everything is energy! We send the impulse into the core of being of the soul, into the primordial power:

*I am the Order in God's All-Order.*

*I am the Order in God's All-Order.*

*I am the Order in God's All-Order.*

Now the Eternal takes another step with us. We again address the All-Order while thinking of our disposition.

Now it is:

*I am the Order in God's All-Order, which illuminates my disposition.*

We speak deep into our soul, into the primordial power:

*I am the Order in God's All-Order, which illuminates my disposition.*

Thoughts and words are energies. Let us think once more into the primordial power:

*I am the Order in God's All-Order, which illuminates my disposition.*

*I am the Order in God's All-Order, which illuminates my disposition.*

With these impulses of the law, we again set the seismograph into motion. The seismograph can be relentless, if we mean to seriously work on ourselves and allow it to point out the programs of our disposition that are not in unison with the divine Order, with our divine heritage.

What will the seismograph bring out in us? What will our consciousness signal to us? Here are just a few examples: Perhaps we will suddenly become aware of our negligence, when we should be helping and supporting the other one, be it at work, when traveling, at home, underway in a vehicle, etc.

Our disposition has recorded, among other things, our wanting to be and to have, which comes from our self-pity, and which expresses itself in a variety of ways. A person with an attitude of expectation suffers from a lack of energy; he is dependent on recognition and aggrandizement from others. People also try to take energy by reproaching or blaming others.

The one who does not see through this theatre of the ego falls for it – and an exchange of energy takes place. And it is not about divine energy here. Being dependent and tied to others to the point of enslavement are the consequences. The stronger ego inflates itself and knows how to adroitly manipulate its fellowman, in order to utilize his energy. The loss of energy of the one who – seemingly voluntarily, and yet only because of his weakness – subordinates himself, subjugates himself, leads to feelings of dejection and depression.

We cannot talk about a fulfilled life for either of the partners in this energy-exchange. Despite his wielding of power, the one will not be happy from within, and the discontented one in the role of the victim will not be happy, either. Feelings of helplessness, self-doubt, impulses of self-negation, giving up on himself to the point of self-destruction darken his disposition. Rebellion, envy, perhaps even hatred toward the domineering one brings out aggression.

Many a one may be able to conceal his aggressive surge of emotions behind a façade of decency and good behavior or even sanctimoniousness and feigned spiritual integrity for a long time. And if he happens to slip out of this role, then he may even know how to disguise it with finesse, by presenting himself to his neighbor with such cleverly devised phrases, that the latter falls into the trap of feeling guilty himself, whereby the one filled with aggression then tries to drain him of energy.

The tendencies of ego-humanness – for instance, envy, jealousy, being self-opinionated, which is the same as being a know-it-all – keep many people's emotions in constant movement. They are negative basic features, programs, from which every person – who wants to raise himself out of the all-too-human baseness into the high consciousness of the Absolute Law – has to recognize and clear out many a thing in himself, even if it is only a small remainder. The intensive path being taught as a gift of grace from God, via the levels of His basic forces, requires the willingness to recognize oneself – expressed differently, it presupposes the willingness to learn on oneself.

As already mentioned, a person who earnestly draws closer to the primordial power increasingly sets his seismograph into motion. However, it is essential that we pay attention to the impulses that come into our consciousness as thoughts or pictures or even feelings, and that we clear up these dissonances, so that from then on, we no longer think, speak or do the same or like things.

Like the Inner Path, this short path of the law begins from without to within. No matter where we may be during the day, no matter what daily work we do, we should make ourselves aware, over and over again, that our true being, the eternal law, our divine heritage, is in the very basis of our soul, into which we think or speak the following impulses again and again:

*I am the Order in God's All-Order,*
*which illuminates my disposition.*

*I am the Order in God's All-Order,*
*which illuminates my disposition.*

As we've read, in time our senses will also begin to react. The seismograph begins to react everywhere, where those things that are not good make themselves at home in us and in our surroundings. In time, it will also stimulate our senses of sight, hearing, smell, taste and touch. The primordial power, the All-Order, will become active in us; it wants us to refine ourselves.

Everything is energy. The all-too-human peculiarities are negative, that is, transformed-down, potentials of energy. They want to be transformed up into divine power, in order to again find their place back in the great totality, in the law of love and unity, as an intensity of radiation. If we become aware of this more often, we will be stimulated to do what is necessary to put order in our emotions. If we continue to do this, we will very soon feel in our disposition, which is cleansing itself, how good it feels to bring things into order externally, and gradually, more and more internally.

Who doesn't want to feel better and more alive, happy and free from within, united with the true life? The primordial power in us, the eternal law, our divine heritage, can do everything – if we, the human being, want this. This means, when we give the divine, the Absolute Law, the possibility to become effective – through our trust, our constant alignment, through our deep desire to grow closer to God.

I repeat some teaching statements from the last lesson: Soon we will then be able to grasp our thoughts more clearly and to more clearly perceive our body's radiation. We will not only become more sensitive toward our own behavior, but also toward our fellowman.

We will also learn to grasp and understand the animal, plant and mineral worlds, yes, all of nature, with a certain delicacy of feeling. Everything is radiation. Every radiation contains the primordial core of divine lawfulness, which strives, yes, even urges us, to remove all our all-too-human aspects without delay, in order to soon become one with our true being.

Dear brothers, dear sisters, this schooling, too, was only a very small insight into the mighty divine law of All-radiation that is the love and unity.

And so, it goes into the very basis of our soul, to our divine heritage. The more often we make an effort to apply the Order of the law, the more purposefully we put order into our surroundings, and also into our disposition, the happier and freer we will be.

Particularly during the present time, the question comes up again and again: Where is the world-ship drifting to? Or: When is it going to go under? – For the spiritually awakened person, the motto is: I save myself and cling resolutely to the anchor of Jesus, the Christ.

Dear brothers and sisters, I wish for all of us, inner joy and inner happiness. May these gifts of inner life fill out our earthly existence.

Whoever keeps to this with God, the Almighty, and His Son, our Redeemer, will begin to truly live; he will develop creative senses and love for the divine deed.

From my heart, I wish all of us a lot, a lot of life!

*Gabi*

*I Am*
*the Order in God's*
*All-Order, which Shines*
*Throughout the Content*
*of My Thoughts.*

Order 3

# *Order 3*

*Dear* brothers and sisters in Christ, further aspects from the Absolute Law of God:

God is love.

The heavenly law, which consists of the seven basic powers, is the highest power – it is the love. Without love, there is no basic power of Order. Without love, there is no basic power of Will, of Wisdom or of Earnestness.

Love is the carrying force, which is also active in the three attributes of filiation – kindness, love and gentleness – which unite the children of God, the sons and daughters of God, with Him, the Father-Mother-God.

The unity of the children of God, the love-energy of the sons and daughters of heaven, flows back again into the heart of God, and at the same time, brings about the creative power in the four natures of Order Will, Wisdom and Earnestness. This magnificent blending of the divine powers is the all-giving power, the love.

As Jesus, Christ proved these fundamental all-cosmic correlations. Out of love for the people and in connection with the primordial power, which is love, He caused a part of His divine heritage to flow. His divine heritage flowed as sparks into all burdened souls, whether they were incarnate or discarnate. And so, each one of us bears in his soul the spark of the Christ of God, the redeeming power, the love, which unites us with the eternal Father.

Each one of us decides when the person or the soul immerses into the absoluteness, into the law of love, the All-ocean of God, and is again home in the eternal homeland.

The cross of resurrection is the sign of divine love. Let us realize that Jesus went to the cross because He loved us human beings. And so, He let Himself be crucified by the powers of darkness. Among other things, He demonstrated with this that despite the crucifixion – and especially because of it – it became apparent that God, the Father-Mother-God, as well as Christ, the Co-regent of the heavens, love all souls and people unendingly. Thus, the cross of resurrection is the sign of love for God and neighbor. Jesus not only taught us the love of our Father; He also personified it right up to the "It is finished," which He spoke on the cross, thus showing us: Victory is His.

Jesus taught us in the following sense: Whoever hears My teaching and does it is a wise man. Every truly wise person has reached the conviction that he must change himself, in order to attain wisdom. This means that he must analyze himself and learn, in order to change toward the positive. True intelligence is a wisdom that has nothing to do with age, but with an attitude toward life. An intelligent, wise person, who painstakingly examines his life on earth each day anew, will recognize that situations, occurrences and also problems concern not only others, but above all, himself. Based on this learning and self-analysis, many a one will realize that the language of the day also concerns him – no matter what the day points out to him.

The right kind of learning means to always look at life from the standpoint of what God wants – not what we, the human being, want.

To gradually come to understand life, which is love, unity, wisdom and freedom, we should always become aware that each one of us is on the path of expanding our consciousness. In order to attain the consciousness, the awareness, for life, we should apply the divine law, which is life, in order to set into motion the seismograph, which can be a very helpful and invaluable traveling companion, if we want to expand our consciousness.

The more often we connect with the primordial power in us, by applying the language of the divine law, that is, by addressing the absolute potential of the primordial power in us, the more often the seismograph will react, pointing out to us during the day – no matter what it brings us – what should be decided and put into practice by us today.

Every person lives in the language of pictures. His thoughts and words are shells, in which, each time, a whole chain of pictures is stored. Since we people talk very fast and most of us are aware only of what we want to say or not say, we repress the pictures that lie in our words. Among other things, we also cannot fully fathom the chain of pictures and, if necessary, express it, because one word leads to another. So we hardly perceive the links of the chain, the various and sundry links, which can also be called sequences of pictures, and thus, these energy formations continue to remain unaware in us. Consequently, most people know themselves only superficially.

A good analyst, who has taken on the task of getting to the bottom of the intrinsic substance of his thoughts and words, knows who he really is. He is also aware that what is going on behind his thoughts and words is he, himself, that is, it shapes his person.

Many, very many, people go through the motions of their day. They do not know their chain of pictures, the content of their feelings, their thoughts and words. For this reason, their deeds and activities are interwoven and influenced by the picture sequences of their content. In himself, the person is often not truthful, but lives in the tension field of his own "for and against" without being aware of this. This leads not only to misunderstandings, but also to wrong judgments and wrong decisions in his personal sphere and to small or large mistakes at work, even to crassly negligent wrongdoings.

A person who is aware of these facts, these dangers, and who dedicates his earthly existence to the life, which is God, cherishes the seismograph, which – if we take it seriously – unmistakably brings everything to the light of day. The seismograph, which is related to the conscience in its function, knows no compromises. However, we humans often put a stop to it. We gloss over the seismograph by placating ourselves with the excuse that the seismograph didn't really mean things the way it brought them out of our soul and our subconscious. So ultimately, we deceive, yes, cheat, ourselves.

The inputs into the Absolute Law, into the primordial power, with which we have begun, are a great turning point in our daily "for and against," and in the excuses that we want to use as our "take-it-easy programs" to counter the seismograph.

The one who earnestly and conscientiously accepts the great and mighty helping hand of our heavenly Father to His human children and purposefully works with it will reach the certainty that this help from God's eternal law not only refines his senses, but also expands and sharpens the awareness of his senses. Through this, he can shape his life on earth ever better, because he knows how to concentrate and, in time, is also able to analyze himself. This brings him increasing insight and discernment into things and events that are being played out in his surroundings and also in this world. He thus grasps much that was closed to him until now or which he faced with indifference and disinterest.

Everything that our senses signal to us wants to tell us something. Our senses send manifold impulses and influence our world of thoughts. To figure out these processes in their individual aspects is, among other things, a part of our personal day, of learning from the energy of our day.

For the one who makes efforts to strive toward his true self, this mighty helping hand of our heavenly Father makes it possible within a short time to not only gain insight into his all-too-human aspects via the seismograph – he will also feel the divine nearness, a deep, transcendent joy, an inner feeling of happiness that triggers an indescribable thankfulness toward our heavenly Father. We feel we have received a gift and we feel fulfilled.

Now I begin with the repetitions of the inputs into the primordial power, into the Absolute Law. Then we will turn to a further input, which God, the primordial power in us, absorbs again, as does our soul and the cell systems of our body. With the decisive affirmations of aspects of the Absolute in us, we bring about a definitive effect on our whole person. From this, the seismograph develops, which is an incorruptible admonisher.

Let us now think deep into our soul, into the primordial power:

*I am the Order in God's All-Order.*

*I am the Order in God's All-Order.*

*I am the Order in God's All-Order.*

*I am the Order in God's All-Order, which illuminates my disposition.*

*I am the Order in God's All-Order, which illuminates my disposition.*

*I am the Order in God's All-Order, which illuminates my disposition.*

Now we go a step further into the Absolute Law, to liberate ourselves from our all-too-human aspects, from our sinfulness.

Again, let us think deep into our soul, into the primordial power:

*I am the Order in God's All-Order,*
*which shines throughout*
*the content of my thoughts.*

*I am the Order in God's All-Order,*
*which shines throughout*
*the content of my thoughts.*

*I am the Order in God's All-Order,*
*which shines throughout*
*the content of my thoughts.*

*I am the Order in God's All-Order,*
*which shines throughout*
*the content of my thoughts.*

The one who uncompromisingly makes great efforts to grow closer to God in his true self will also find a hold in himself, with God in him.

Our unstable time is growing darker and darker, because people's dispositions and moods are growing ever darker. For everyone thinks solely of himself, in order to save his own skin. Only the fewest think about saving their soul, of helping it become more light-filled, in order to enter the true paradise, after the death of their body, to enter our eternal homeland, which is our land of origin.

Many people seek salvation in the temporal, whereby they become ever more insecure. For this reason, aggressions and inhuman acts of violence and riots are increasing, excesses against one's neighbor, but also against the animals and the Mother Earth. People's instability worldwide, their brutal acts of violence, bring about the destruction of the planet Earth and not lastly, the extermination of the human race.

Therefore, again and again the motto:
May the one who wants to save himself, save himself!

I repeat: May the one who wants to save himself, save himself! The anchor has been given – it is the teachings of Jesus, the Christ. The person who holds fast to the anchor of the divine laws will not go under. His path is the path with Christ to the eternal light, to the peace and the secureness that comes from the heavenly Father, who wants to have His children by His heart again.

Dear brothers, dear sisters, the more often we apply the Order of the law, the more often we put order in our surroundings and in our disposition and our thoughts as well, the more happy and free we will be.

Let us wish us all, a lot of spiritual, inner success, which leads to a lot, a lot of life!

United in the love for God and neighbor,
Your sister,
*Gabi*

*I* Am
*the Order in God's
All-Order, which Makes
Manifest the Content
of My Words.*

Order 4

# *Order 4*

*D*ear brothers, dear sisters in Christ, from the mighty helping hand of our eternal Father, let us read the next large step towards the primordial power, the absolute cosmic law, which is the love for God and neighbor.

God, our eternal Father, and Christ, our Redeemer, show us different ways we can return to our land of origin, to our eternal homeland, in the brief time that remains.

The direct large step is to draw closer to the primordial power, God's love, in the depths of our soul, in order to again find our way into unity, peace and secureness. The love for God and neighbor is the heavenly power that unites all beings and all pure forces of infinity.

Jesus, the Christ, spoke of the Kingdom of God, which is within, in us. The Kingdom of God in us is the kingdom of love, because the heart of all Being is God's love. The love for God and neighbor is the central light, which shines throughout our true being, illuminating it. Through the love for God and neighbor, those people who strive toward the One, who is God, our Father, and who loves each one of us unendingly, are one with and among one another.

Many people say the words "love for God and neighbor" and, in the last analysis, don't know what love for God and neighbor means. For those who are willing to open their heart to the love for God and neighbor, I want to first draw from our divine heritage, from our true being, which is love, and try to put into words what shows us the way to our land of origin.

Love heals the wounds of the soul – when a person professes to the love for God and has the desire to unfold in himself the love, the selflessly giving power.

Where there is suffering, love wants to comfort.

Where hopelessness prevails, love wants to give hope and the strength to develop step by step from the negative to the positive.

Love links those people who build on God.

Love gives the lonely unity in community, in the love for God and neighbor – if the person wants this.

Love gives secureness through the power of love, which unites everything pure, everything ethically worthwhile.

All beautiful, noble things come forth from love. Works of love create harmony, accord, true understanding and true brotherliness among one another.

Love brings freedom.
Love is peaceful.
Love builds and develops.
Love is inextinguishable trust
and spiritual closeness, spiritual union.
Love is the hope in the dark world.

And so, God's love unites all pure forces, from the interaction of which grow further gifts of love. God's love is the power of becoming and growing, the serving, giving, selfless, impersonal force that leads everything toward the good.

The so-called law of the Fall, the causal law and causality, which binds and thus, makes one unfree, developed as a result of the wrong, unlawful thinking, speaking and acting that directed itself against the power of love, and still does. Through causality, people are bound to each other who have created the same and similar causes, that is, who have indebted themselves with the un-good.

The causal law could also be called the law of egoism. The self-centeredness of the ego allows no selfless giving and serving. The egotistical person is driven by wanting to be and to have. He strives for his advantage; he takes, that is, robs, the energy of others. And so, the person who turns against the love for God and neighbor makes of himself – spiritually and physically – a personal causal law. He, himself, creates his causes; and so, the effect is also *his* fate. The person determines himself and thus, is his own law.

In the pure Being, in the eternal Kingdom of God, every being is the Absolute Law, which is love. Consequently, all divine beings are one amongst each other and are merged in the law of God, in love. And all beings of love are one with all pure forces of the Being, a part of which is the heavenly nature kingdoms and the large and small animals in their immeasurable multiplicity.

The sole power, the All-power, is love for God and neighbor. It lasts eternally. It also streams throughout the Fall-realms, the earthly nature kingdoms and the earth itself. In the world, in everything created from man's self-will, it is often latent, as is the immortal positive core. The divine love softens and links the hearts of people who surrender to the Father-Mother-love, which is the love for God and neighbor.

The law of God leaves to every person the freedom to decide for the life, which is love, or for the love that is focused on a person. This brings in its wake transience, loneliness, suffering and need, everything causal that the person inflicted upon himself, and still does.

Because God, our heavenly Father, loves us immeasurably, He points out, and His Son, Jesus, the Christ, our Redeemer, points out, again and again, the ways that lead to love, to the primordial power, to the eternal homeland. His desire and His will is that many soon awaken in His consciousness, in His law, of love.

A further step toward the liberating love for God and neighbor is the purification of our words. We know meanwhile that the "seismograph" is an invaluable companion during our day. I want to briefly repeat the already known steps toward the primordial power, in order to point out the next step.

And so, we first think deep into our soul, into the primordial power:

*I am the Order in God's All-Order.*

*I am the Order in God's All-Order,*
*which illuminates my disposition.*

*I am the Order in God's All-Order,*
*which shines throughout the content of my thoughts.*

I repeat:
*I am the Order in God's All-Order.*

*I am the Order in God's All-Order,*
*which illuminates my disposition.*

*I am the Order in God's All-Order,*
*which shines throughout the content of my thoughts.*

Now follows the next step toward the primordial power, toward the love for God and neighbor.

We again think deeply, very deeply, into our soul:

*I am the Order in God's All-Order,*
*which makes manifest*
*the content of my words.*

*I am the Order in God's All-Order,*
*which makes manifest*
*the content of my words.*

*I am the Order in God's All-Order,*
*which makes manifest*
*the content of my words.*

Dear brothers and sisters, it is a known fact that we human beings talk too much, as well as talking about unessential things. For whatever reason we do it, a part of our law of egoism is always there. We want to show off, for instance, or hide our insecurity or cover up our inferiority complex. The seismograph, which accompanies us on the way to the primordial power – insofar as we let it – and which points out our egoism to us, will also admonish us in situations when we talk too much about inessential things. At the same time, it reveals to us *why* we are acting this way.

If we give the seismograph free access to the content of our words, if we take seriously what it reveals, which either shows itself in a sequence of pictures or expresses itself in our disposition, and if we correct the egocentric content of our words, we will become calmer, more peaceful and more certain in dealing with our fellowman. Yes, our choice of words changes. And the rhythm of our speech also refines, because the content of our words is carried more and more by the law of love for God and neighbor.

If we make use of the helping hand of our heavenly Father by taking this wonderful path, then our life on earth will soon change to the positive. The inner freedom that we gain through this leads to farsightedness and the ability to see all around us. We become more free toward our fellowman at work; assessments and value-judgments recede. We feel ever more deeply into our daily life, in order to help and serve others. Through this, we become more open; we master problems and worries and contribute to solutions being found that correspond to the will of God. Our work is more purposeful and balanced. And in the family and among friends, we are more reconciliatory, more receptive and helpful. Yes, we become a more valuable friend and companion who meets his neighbor with understanding and tolerance.

And so, if we allow what God wants, we gain a lot, a lot of life!

Dear brothers and sisters in the Spirit of our Redeemer, in this sense, a heartfelt and divine greeting,

*Gabi*

*I Am the Life
in God's Work of the Deed,
in His Creation for People, Nature
and Animals.*

Order 5

# Order 5

*D*ear brothers, dear sisters in Christ, the Spirit of our heavenly Father is the life. God alone is good. Our heavenly Father, kindness itself, wants us to be totally with Him, at His bosom, the ocean of life. His infinitely eternal power, the love, shines more intensely into this world through His Son, Christ, the Co-Regent of the heavens.

Especially during this time on earth, the light of the Christ of God flows particularly strongly around the earthball. His light, His word of revelation, which goes out over the whole world via radio and television, is one-of-a-kind in all of the Fall-event.

Many a one among us notices that something has come into movement. He sees it, with one look into this world, where disasters are increasingly piling up, where violence and many different kinds of base instincts are running riot, which is shown particularly in the exploitation and cheating of those who are weaker, but above all, in the unscrupulous and cruel crimes committed against nature, Mother Earth and the animal world. Many people act ever more brutally against their fellowman and the animals. Although, by far, not everything is reported in the media whoever knows how to read between the lines grasps the unbelievable extent of the evil that is expressed in many different kinds of abnormal and repulsive acts. The evil seed, sown over thousands of years – the guilt that has not been expiated or paid off – is now sprouting. The fruits of evil are becoming visible. The harvest is in full swing.

Whatever does not vibrate in the law of God, what does not correspond to His Order, now exposes itself; it comes to light. This development does not stop at the door of the church institutions, either. The evil, the dirt under the so-called "holy" robes, becomes apparent; consternation awakens many a church sheep from its sleep. The church that consistently pretends to be honorable is suffering a progressively accelerated loss of confidence among the population everywhere across the earth. Here, too, the fate that has only itself to blame for is running its course. This is not surprising, considering that the caste of priests principally is to blame for the disasters that Mother Earth has to bear and endure.

But an alert contemporary also feels and registers the power of the eternal Spirit, the stream of divine light, that flows inexorably into the deepest spheres of the Fall. The Christ of God radiates, radiates and radiates. He radiates over the whole earth; He radiates into the continents and into the hearts of all those people who are prepared to listen to His word and to take the steps toward Him, Christ.

The unique chance is offered to each one, to still put behind himself a significant part of the way on the Inner Path that leads back to God in the eternal homeland, during the days left before this world passes away. Jesus, the Christ, however, will not be able to reach all people, because they are only listeners of the words of God, forgetting the deeds of love.

For thousands of years, the forces that have turned away from God have worked on this earth to the effect that people think and act against God's Order, against His law of love, against His unity of creation. Unfortunately, even today, many have been shaped by the caste of priests. They knew and still know how to cleverly hide their base motives and ambitions behind a shining mask and sonorous words. Church functionaries still continue to have an influence on those who blindly follow them. Their unwholesome, even corrupting, fall-out has an effect on the hearts and in the consciousness of many people. Way too many still listen to the caste of priests. Until today, people follow their herd instinct and fall for their beautiful-sounding, yet empty words.

Christ is the law of life of the good. He lived what He taught. He taught the peace, the brotherliness in the love for God and for neighbor. This is the inner Christianity that should be expressed externally in all areas of life, and which should flow into the Kingdom of Peace on earth.

Many a one does not see that the Prince of Peace, Jesus, the Christ, is being marketed in the most shameful and base ecclesiastical, institutional way. At most, the true Christian values like equality, freedom, unity, brotherliness and justice cross their lips. But the only thing that counts with the caste of priests is to keep their sinecure, their prestige and their wealth.

Despite this unlawfulness that opens up more and more and brings this world to plunge into the abyss, the light of love is flowing more and more on the earth, into this world, to those people who are of good will. Whoever is able to observe and to analyze the disaster of this world recognizes that we human beings are standing before a mighty turn of time, into which the Spirit of God is very gradually putting things into order. The cosmic timespan of probation is drawing to an end.

The call of the Christ of God is sounding out worldwide. He calls over and over again: May the one who wants to save himself, save himself, before this world passes away!

Many of us know that the saving anchor is Christ alone, our Redeemer in God, our Father, the primordial power, the light in the very basis of the soul of every person, as well as in every discarnate soul that is in the spheres of purification.

I would like to repeat again, to give ourselves the possibility to let it fall deep into our hearts, so that it touches our heart: As never before in the history of mankind, the light of God radiates into this time all over the earth, inexorably, continuously and with a power that has no equal. A mighty Christ-atmosphere has formed through the intense divine radiation that has taken place over the decades, a potential of highest spiritual energy, that was already partly built up by the prophets of the Old Covenant and above all, by Jesus, the Christ, through His Redeemer-deed. This shining atmospheric layer is like a cosmic band of rays that have formed around the Mother Earth and increasingly intensifies – a pathway of light, on which Christ, the Co-Regent of the heavens, journeys to the earth in order to raise into the primordial radiation, into the spiritual, into the consciousness of the divine All-life, everything that the earth still bears until His spiritual return.

The one who takes a close look at this world with alert eyes recognizes that the divine principle is active: Countless species of animals are being taken back. Their ray of life or their part-souls are returning to their divine consciousness, in order to continue living and developing in the All-cosmos, according to their spirit consciousness. Over the course of the time of Order on this earth, ever more people will also pass away. Ever fewer souls will incarnate, among other things, because it is no longer possible for them. For an earth that has been raised by Christ, that has become more light-filled through the principle of Order, will now give shelter to only that which is light-filled and will bear only so many people, animals and plant species as corresponds to the garden of God, a light-filled earth.

Once the Christ of God has raised the radiation of the earth, then the divine Order on earth has been accomplished for the most part. And then the question is: Which person fulfills the will of God?

And so, it can be said that we human beings are still in a time rich with opportunities. Although God's All-Order has been active on earth for a certain length of time, the Spirit of our heavenly Father in Christ, our Redeemer, still gives us the opportunity to put order in our life on earth, and to shape it anew, that is, spiritually, in order to draw closer to our eternal homeland, and above all, to God, our eternal Father.

Let us become aware of the fact that it is Christ alone who is the help for each one of us. He is our salvation, because He knows each one of us. He knows about us. He, alone, is the way into the Father's house. The one who lets himself be guided, Christ takes by the hand. He invites each one of us to take seriously the instructions of His Father, who is the Father of us all, in order to get out of the dangerous chaos of the world. It is only the Spirit of the Christ of God who knows how long this world will still exist. But He admonishes and admonishes. And the one who takes His admonishments seriously is aware that this is a grave time and every hour is precious.

Many people have already received many impulses from the Spirit of God. Now, He once again extends His hand to us. The direct road to life is shown to us, the Order in God's All-Order is revealed to us, which we can apply in our daily life, above all, on ourselves.

We now come to the All-Order in the work of the deed of God, which is the unity in the work of creation of the Almighty. A human being does not do justice to the divine work of creation by merely including the principle of divine All-Order in the work of his personal daily life, but by aligning himself with the work of God, which is the love for God and neighbor. This is to be actualized not only at his place of work but also in neighborly love for all people, for all animals, for all living beings and living forms that are borne by Mother Earth, as well as for the elemental forces that are a part of the earth.

However, before we come to the All-Order in the work of the deed of God, I would like to briefly call to mind the cosmic tasks already given, which we now let flow deep into our soul, into the primordial power. They are:

*I am the Order in God's All-Order.*

*I am the Order in God's All-Order, which illuminates my disposition.*

*I am the Order in God's All-Order, which shines throughout the content of my thoughts.*

*I am the Order in God's All-Order, which makes manifest the content of my words.*

I repeat:

*I am the Order in God's All-Order.*

*I am the Order in God's All-Order, which illuminates my disposition.*

*I am the Order in God's All-Order, which shines throughout the content of my thoughts.*

*I am the Order in God's All-Order, which makes manifest the content of my words.*

Now follows the next step nearer to God in us. It is:

*I am the life in God's work of the deed,*
*in His creation, for people, nature*
*and animals.*

Let us again intensely think these words deep into our inner being, into the innermost part of our soul:

*I am the life in God's work of the deed,*
*in His creation, for people, nature*
*and animals.*

I may again repeat:

*I am the life in God's work of the deed,*
*in His creation, for people, nature*
*and animals.*

Dear brothers, dear sisters in Christ, these truly are words of life, for they are spoken to us people from the divine unity.

We human beings should become aware of the fact that God is love and unity. This growing awareness lets us recognize how short-sighted we were – and perhaps still are – if we only revolve around the little world of our senses, that sees and perceives only ourselves and perhaps reaches as far as our family or our colleagues at work.

Let us train our senses by ever more often during the day making ourselves aware of the thoughts of Order of love and neighborly love: "I am the life in God's work of the deed, in His creation, for people, nature and animals" – and then the inner "seismograph" will also show us where our world of the senses presently is. The admonisher and giver of impulses that we call our "seismograph" will advise us to realize whether we are still bound to our little, personal world, or whether we already look a little beyond our bindings. Then we will entrust ourselves to Christ, extending our hand to Him, so that He can guide us to the eternal Father, to the life, to the primordial power, to our true being, deep in the very basis of our soul.

Please, dear brothers, dear sisters, do not leave the seismograph out of consideration. It could be an invaluable companion, because via our feelings and via our conscience it draws our attention to what we are still bound to, where the lack of freedom still holds us captive.

May I encourage you, all of us, to leave the prison, the dungeon of self-will, of being a loner? For in the true life, in the All-life of God, shines the Primordial Light that wants to encompass us, to protect and guide us; it is the Christ of God, who waits for us and is calling to us: May the one who wants to save himself, save himself, before this world passes away!

*I am the life in God's work of the deed,
in His creation, for people, nature
and animals.*

What significance particularly this new sentence with which we address the Absolute Law in us has for us becomes clear when we become aware of the following:

The universal work of the great God, His glorious creation, would never have reached completion, would never have been able to grow and take on new form, if God, the Creator of all Being, had left it at the creation thought, at the word. According to what is written, however, we can read, "God spoke ... and it was ..." It was, that is, it became. The deed followed the word. Based on His word, the All-creation of the Being emerged.

If we want to, we can take a quiet hour to think about the following: What makes a person invaluable? Is it his words, or is it his deeds? Of what use is it, if a person merely talks with nice words, utters only great words of high value – but doesn't act accordingly?

Again I want to bring to life for us the words of liberation, that mean love and unity:

Again, we think into our soul, deep into the very basis of our soul:

*I am the life in God's work of the deed,*
*in His creation, for people, nature*
*and animals.*

*I am the life in God's work of the deed,*
*in His creation, for people, nature*
*and animals.*

*I am the life in God's work of the deed,*
*in His creation, for people, nature*
*and animals.*

Dear brothers, dear sisters, let us accept the helping hand of the eternal Spirit of love that is reaching out to us, that alone is good! His kindness points out to us once again the wonderful and direct pathway, so that we can change our life on earth to the positive in a short time. We do not lose anything – we gain much!

We gain inner freedom and openness. We experience the sensitivity of our senses. We attain farsight and insight and live in the commandment of the hour that is the love for God and neighbor. We learn to sense deeply and grasp much more during our daily living. Through this, we can also help and serve others. We work out solutions to problems and worries, solutions that correspond to the will of God. We begin to live more consciously; we will work more consciously at our place of work. We become more conciliatory, receptive and helpful toward our fellowman.

Invaluable people are so rare today. But whoever knows he goes at the hand of the Christ of God will become an invaluable friend and companion, a person of love for God and neighbor, who practices understanding and tolerance toward his fellowmen. The one who opens his heart for the life does what God wants. He senses that the eternal life pulsates in him. With joy and thankfulness, he will then say: I gain more and more, a lot, a lot of life!

In this awareness, dear brothers and sisters, a very warm and divine greeting!

*Gabi*

*I Am the Will*
*in God's Will of Creation*
*that Brightens My Disposition*
*and Is the Content*
*of My Thoughts.*

Will 1

# Will 1

Dear brothers, dear sisters in Christ, let us read the message of divine love and wisdom.

Whoever looks into this world with alert eyes sees and experiences that, in all four points of direction, the East, West, South and North, this world lies in a quagmire of sin, for disaster, starvation and pestilence are reaching out to each other, as it were.

Despite these many indications that this world is heading toward the abyss and that parts of it have already fallen, many people still believe the beguiling and soothing speeches of the politicians who are trying to color black as white. Unfortunately, many people are not capable of analyzing the messages of world disasters and the polished speeches of the politicians. So many a one believes what is dished out to him. He thinks it is the truth. But in reality, it is only a snare adorned with hopeful aphorisms to disguise its real intent.

While taking a closer look, an analytical mind recognizes that the indifferent person without a will of his own is to be tied to the statements of the politicians, who still lead people to believe in a better, future world. There is talk of an upward trend in the economy – that fits with the pipe-dream of many – and which says: More money for a fun-loving life. These snares not only ignore the all-prevailing Spirit, His absolute Will, but also ignore – above all – the fact that the earth and the elemental forces simply react differently than what the governing authorities would have people believe. However this whitewashing will soon prove to be an illusion. The actual state of blackness will come to the fore again. For the politicians, as well as the church representatives, of whom it is known that they sit in one boat, as well as all those who pay homage to both ego parties of politics and church, not only ignore the Will of God, His holy law, but deliberately place themselves against the Will of God and His creation.

The vast majority of the "great" of this world, to whom the people look up, the gods of idolatry, ignore the fact that they themselves are not the Creator of the earth nor of creation. Such and similar idolatrous deformities presume to act against the One whose All-radiation has long since announced the disintegration of this world.

With the word "world," we are not referring to the planet Earth, whose shining core of being is a part of the pure Being. The "world" is rather the fabric of human disorder that is built on egoism. It is characterized by lust for power, control, oppression, exploitation and violence.

God's All-power, the All-life, His holy law, is radiating ever more intensely into the disorder, into the disaster of this world. For, at the end of the existence of all human impudence, stands once and for all: God's work according to His holy Will, to His Absolute Law. What stands in His way ultimately destroys itself.

The human being has forgotten what the commandments of God and the teachings of Jesus, the Christ, want to tell us. These lawful principles say that when this world passes away, God in Christ will be the Victor over the diabolical experts who until today continue to be of the opinion that they can improve on God's works.

We human beings are in a mighty time of change. The law of God introduces the New Era, the era of the Spirit. God has spoken the "Let there be": There will be a new heaven and a new earth. He did not speak about this world and the state of this world. And so, God does not include these in His "Let there be." This is why we have the call of Jesus, the Christ: May the one who wants to save himself, save himself, before this world passes away!

The word of the Almighty in Christ, our Redeemer, streams in fullness over the earth. It can be heard and read on all continents in many different languages. Christ, our Redeemer, the Co-Regent of the Heavens, accepts every willing person in order to guide him into the inner life, and then lead his soul to the heavenly Father, who waits with great longing for His beloved child, His beloved son, His beloved daughter. Christ reaches out to us. He does this very specially through the Inner Path to God in the very center of our soul, for the Kingdom of God, our true, eternal homeland, is in us as essence, power and light.

The path within is the path into happiness, into freedom and health, for when the soul grows lighter, the cells of our body are awash with the life that is God.

God is light.

Let us allow the light of God to shine in our soul and in the cells of our body, and then we will feel fresher, more buoyant, happier, more hopeful and healthier into old age. The path to a life that makes us free can be followed by every person, a young person as well as an older person. There is no age in God, instead, for the physical body, there is freshness, youth and spontaneity, until, in this spirit, in the spirit of a sunny and joyful true life that brings happiness, the life continues in the fine-material world. There, the soul of a thoroughly light-filled person then journeys toward the One whom he served in love and thankfulness while a human being. He, the great All-One, gave the person the freshness, the health, the glad and hopeful years and then guided his soul into the beyond, into the life that lasts eternally.

If God has become the shining center of our thinking and of our behavior, in that we strive toward the fulfillment of the lawful principles of life, we will increasingly be thankful for His word of primordial power, and happy that we may receive this, beginning with the divine Order.

Ever more people long for the word of the primordial power, the word of law from God that leads us to within, into the Kingdom of Peace, into the eternal homeland that knows no shadows and in which the Primordial Light shines, irradiating all beings and all Being.

Since ever more people make this need known, directing their request to Universal Life, to repeat the Primordial Light, the path of law, I gladly do it.

And so, we will first call to mind in us the Primordial Light, which then shows us our further steps. This will be a joy for the one who has fulfilled for the most part the indications of Order from the law of the infinitely eternal Being.

I repeat:

*I am the Order in God's All-Order.*

*I am the Order in God's All-Order,*
*which illuminates my disposition.*

*I am the Order in God's All-Order,*
*which shines throughout the content of my thoughts.*

*I am the Order in God's All-Order,*
*which makes manifest the content of my words.*

*I am the Life in God's work of the deed,*
*in His creation, for people, nature and animals.*

Now follows the next step, which addresses the Will of God in us, in our disposition and in our thoughts.

Dear brothers, dear sisters, the true life shines in the very basis of our soul; it is God, the Primordial Light. This is why we sink into the Christ-of-God center that pulsates in the proximity of our heart, for the Eternal and Christ are one, *one* Spirit, *one* light, divine power, love and wisdom.

Let us take into our hearts the announced next step that leads to the divine Will. I will repeat it several times.

It says:

*I am the Will in God's*
*Will of creation that brightens my disposition*
*and is the content of my thoughts.*

*I am the Will in God's*
*Will of creation that brightens my disposition*
*and is the content of my thoughts.*

*I am the Will in God's*
*Will of creation that brightens my disposition*
*and is the content of my thoughts.*

Let us once again allow this sentence from the All-Law of the Eternal to flow deeply into our heart, yes, into our soul, in the absolute affirmation:

*I am the Will in God's*
*Will of creation that brightens my disposition*
*and is the content of my thoughts.*

Dear brothers, dear sisters, at this point, I want to call attention to the seismograph that is an invaluable companion, particularly in addressing the law. It raises the deeper layers of our consciousness and subconscious, so that we may follow this wonderful life-path conscientiously and steadfastly. It helps us to see more deeply, so that we do not delude ourselves in terms of our spiritual development. And so, the seismograph is an investigator of the deeper layers of our inputs in our consciousness, in our subconscious and in our soul.

It conveys to us who we still really are, from a human perspective, and what we have input into the repository planets, the purification planes.

Whoever lets the seismograph work without his all-too-human "ifs and buts" or "That's not true, I'm not like that at all!", for him, each day will become an experience of self. He will experience what he really still is like without glossing over it. This can be a quite painful, perhaps even shocking, experience. But of what use is it to shut off the investigators, the seismographs, or to defend oneself against them! We are the ones who input our feeling, thinking, speaking and acting that are far from God, that are against the love for God and neighbor. At some point in time, our egocentric wanting comes to the fore, either in this earthly existence or in a further incarnation. Or we will experience our still existing egotism when we have set aside our physical body and go to the purification planes that, in their vibration, are in accord with our active inputs, staying there as souls.

Jesus, the Christ, speaks His word into our soul, and it is: May the one who wants to save himself, save himself, before this world passes away. These, His words, say a lot. In any case, they tell us: We cannot afford any spiritual idleness; we should take our life on earth in hand so that Christ can lead us. If we follow His offer, we will take secure steps forward, led and guided by Him, on the path of life to the Absolute Life that is God, the love.

In the realization that we should use our time on earth in order to follow the life-path to God, our Father, I repeat the law-step that is another light for us on the path to the true life, a light that shines for us and on us, if we want. And so, I repeat the words so that they gain access to our inner being:

*I am the Will in God's*
*Will of creation that brightens my disposition*
*and is the content of my thoughts.*

*I am the Will in God's*
*Will of creation that brightens my disposition*
*and is the content of my thoughts.*

*I am the Will in God's*
*Will of creation that brightens my disposition*
*and is the content of my thoughts.*

Dear brothers, dear sisters, to gain life means to experience God, for God is life.

In this awareness – to gain life, in order to experience God – I wish you, yes, all of us, that God be and remain the shining and delightful center of our disposition, of our thoughts and words. The highest gain in our earthly existence comes from this. It is: a lot, a lot of life!

A very deeply felt and divine greeting!

*Gabriele*

*I Am the Will*
*in His Will of Creation*
*of the Let There Be.*
*Let There Be More and More Light*
*in My Consciousness.*
*My Five Senses Brighten.*

Will 2

# Will 2

$\mathscr{D}$ear brothers and sisters in Christ, how does the person fare who reads for the first time: "God is the Absolute Law"? Will he, perhaps, shy away a bit from the term "law"? For this reason, it should be said once again what kind of law God is:

All in all, God's law is the love, the love for God and for neighbor. God's law is the life, the unceasing, streaming life. God's law, is therefore, flowing light, the Primordial Light – the highest, infinite power, wisdom and kindness; because God is good.

When we address aspects of the Absolute Law, we are addressing the Primordial Light that is the eternal life in the innermost recesses of our soul.

The spirit of our heavenly Father reaches out His hand to us in a further schooling that addresses the Absolute Law.

God, the Eternal, gives us this unique schooling, so that we can expand our consciousness, our awareness, with the strength of the Primordial Light. Then, very gradually, our five senses are refined: We experience the omnipresent life more consciously and intensely.

Our five senses can be compared to antennas. If our senses are oriented to the world, to the all-too-human, we perceive only external things and situations – and of them, only those that have been stored by the low-vibrating, physical five senses. This means that the five senses are coarser, because they are attuned only to matter and to certain aspects of the earthly existence, which we have registered in our world-oriented consciousness.

And so, our state of consciousness gives our senses the direction. If our state of consciousness is low, this means, focused on this world and on the egotistical and human, then, the sensory perception is restricted accordingly; it is pre-programmed to the world of material phenomena. And then, we perceive only what corresponds to our daily thoughts.

On the other hand, if our consciousness is oriented to God, the All-Emitter, the Primordial Light, to the Spirit of God, then our senses become refined. We feel more finely. We perceive more and grasp deeper inter-relationships, including what takes place in the world of nature and the animals.

If we have oriented our consciousness toward the cosmos, that is, if God, the Spirit, the life, is active in our feelings, sensations, thoughts, words and actions, then we have a very broad sending and receiving potential. We see things more deeply, we hear things that are not perceivable to a limited consciousness. We smell and taste according to the inner guidance and will eat consciously, because the life is also present in food.

If our consciousness is in communication with the mighty All-Emitter, GOD, our senses can be compared to a cosmic radarscope that can listen into the All; it absorbs the gentle stirrings of nature and the animal world, which we then perceive. The fine, cosmic radar-scope of our senses also sounds out the words of our fellowman as well, and from the behavior, the body posture, the gestures, the facial expression, from the total appearance of a person, it perceives the person's basic attitude.

Whoever has reached this high state of divine consciousness will no longer judge or condemn. Why? Because he has taken the steps of awareness that bring him out of the dungeon of "the other is to blame" or "the other is such a blockhead," and has found his way into the consciousness of impersonal life.

We hear over and over again in the programs of the Primordial Light that this wonderful and unique path of schooling is a short, but intensive path, so as to draw closer to the All-life, the Primordial Light, GOD, before this world passes away.

When we look into this chaotic world, we realize that everything, but everything, is coming apart at the seams. And what we read, hear and see via the media is only a fraction of what really is going on. All good values are becoming worthless; all good customs and morals are crumbling away more and more. People are becoming more and more brutal. Just as most people act against their fellowman, they also act against the world of animals and plants, against the Mother Earth.

The consciousness of many people is becoming ever narrower, the state of their consciousness ever lower. Most people think only of themselves, striving only to see how they can save their skin and their belongings – and, at that, often without consideration of whether their fellowman is disadvantaged or even harmed by this.

In reality, nothing can last anymore. If physical strength fades away through illness, hardship, infirmity and hunger, then property, possessions and wealth, which many people depend on, are of no use. You cannot buy your life with money. This is why, while addressing the Absolute Law of God in the Primordial Light, we say: May the one who wants to save himself, save himself!

Many a one thinks that he was disadvantaged by life. From childhood on, he felt the yoke of an earthly existence, the lack of means to enjoy life as so many others do. And if we ask: "Who, specifically, gives us the disadvantage?" most people name their parents. Looking for someone to blame, those who feel self-regret may think of other people or of fate, for which God is then supposedly to blame. And then we often hear about how severe and harsh God is, how hard He is with His Commandments, that He has imposed upon man.

But whoever gets to know the laws of life more and more, and looks at the Ten Commandments more closely, senses that God does not determine and impose on others. For He always says "you shall" and not "you must." So, who spoke out this "must" over us? – We, ourselves! We have thought and spoken to ourselves everything that we may be struggling with in this life on earth.

Those who know about reincarnation also are aware of the fact that each day, at every hour, minute or even moment, each person is working on his "blueprint" for a potentially new incarnation of his soul. We develop this blueprint with the contents of our feelings, sensations, thoughts, words and actions. The contents, the body of our works, determine what kind of inputs these are. In their sum total, they characterize our human character, our human attitude.

All the expressions of our life – including feelings, sensations and thoughts – are energy forms. Since no energy is ever lost, we enter the energy that goes out from us, on the one hand, into the current state of our cells, and, on the other hand, into our soul – and via our soul, we create a matrix in the material universe. This matrix is, so to speak, the blueprint for our next physical body. Our blueprint contains all the factors that will become effective in our new life on earth.

If the soul again goes to earth after the death of our body, into a new incarnation, then what it brings with it and what course its life on earth will take is not by chance. Rather, it brings with itself whatever forms of energy it had created in previous incarnations, that is, as a former human being. Perhaps it may bring, among other things, positive, light-filled energy potentials, but these do not carry any of the heaviness of the earth in themselves.

Above all, it is the negativities that have been registered and stored, that is, the egocentric human aspects, which can draw a soul into a further incarnation. They are the sinful programs, the guilt – briefly stated, the sins. These are what the soul now could and should clear up as a human being in this existence on earth.

So via the energetic matrixes that we have created ourselves and that are called the blueprint, we incarnate and become the child of those people with whom we are connected at the moment of the procreation of our body and the emergence of ourselves as a human being, through the characteristics of the guilty, sinful inputs in our soul. We call these people our parents.

Our "blueprint," which determines the course of our life on earth, is, as stated, not by chance, nor is who procreated us and gave birth to us. It is no coincidence which people we encounter and which people we have something to do with in this life on earth.

As a human being, we can change our blueprint to the positive or negative, improve it or worsen it. Both possibilities lie, in turn, in our hands. During our young years, once we are able to distinguish between good and bad, we already begin to influence the shape and form of our inner and outer life situations that we brought with us.

It is not at all so that a soul, which is born into a rich family, has a more light-filled blueprint, and that the soul, which comes to simple parents, is burdened. Basically, it all depends only on what the individual makes of his life, how he deals with the situations of his life: whether he uses them, in order to gain higher ethical moral values, or whether he lowers the spiritual-moral standards for his life. And the one who, in the course of his life on earth, acquires money and property – regardless of how and what kind – need not think that with this, he has improved the life-line that he previously had drawn up for himself. It has only and alone to do with the person's basic attitude, that has grown from the contents that he placed into his feelings, sensations and thoughts, as well as into his words, into his whole behavior.

Even if a person did many a wrong thing during his youth or in his early adult years, perhaps even adding onto an existing guilt – in later years, a person who has grown more mature can at any time decide to remedy something and re-shape his life. Such a change often triggers the individual suddenly becoming aware of his responsibility, for example. Often, these are drastic changes in the course of his life or so-called blows of fate that bring the person to self-reflection and a re-orientation. Many a one then turns to higher values and ideals. By becoming aware and working on himself, he changes the contents of his feelings, sensations, of his thoughts, words and actions for the positive, thus giving the life, that is God, more room in his life.

So that people are able to achieve this, God gave them the Ten Commandments through Moses and the teachings from the law of life through Jesus, as a help for their spiritual orientation and as a guideline for a truly meaningful life.

Especially worthy of mention, in relation to shaping our life in the spirit of the love for God and neighbor, are the simple – yet applicable in all areas of life – words of Jesus, the Christ, in His Sermon on the Mount: "Do unto others, as you would have them do unto you." Insofar as the person keeps this and uses it to recognize himself and to change the way he leads his life, it can contribute to a quick and deep improvement in the quality of his life, his "blueprint" for his present life on earth.

Whoever works on himself in such a way has Christ, his Redeemer and companion, at His side. God does not forsake us human beings. He is always present. When we turn to Him, pray with our heart to Him and entrust ourselves to Him, we experience His help.

Dear brothers, dear sisters, let us not allow it to come down to perhaps having to experience and learn in old age those things that we thought and spoke toward ourselves during earlier days on earth! This is shown by the fact that we, for example, become sickly, frail or even laid low; or that we can hardly curb our thoughts of hatred and envy; or that we fall into old patterns of sarcasm, which we had thoughtlessly cultivated over the decades; or that we spitefully look down on others or think or talk about them in a contemptuous way; or that we no longer can master our assertiveness toward younger people, which keeps breaking through, and much more.

Once we have grown older, we experience – simply based on our life-film running backwards – our blueprint every now and then. It literally breaks through our disposition, through our weakened cells and indicates who we still are in terms of our human traits, and what we have input since our youth as wrongdoings, wrong attitudes and negative patterns of thought.

Let us be aware that Jesus, the Christ, is always the Savior, at every age of a person, in every situation, in everything that the day reflects to us. He calls us, over and over again, to turn back and change our ways, to reshape and form our lifestyle anew, so that the five senses are refined and our character, which is also our blueprint, becomes more light-filled and sunny.

I would like to repeat here, once more, what the Spirit has given to us in the previous Primordial Light radiations of love and of life, and which make that person more light-filled and sunny who applies this absolute affirmation in his daily life.

Together, let us think deeply into our inner being, into our body. With our light-filled thoughts, we touch the cells of our body, so that we gradually experience the presence of God!

Let us be aware of the fact that the Spirit of God is light in the very basis of our soul. His holy law is light.

Now, I will repeat the words of light, which Jesus, the Christ, gave us, in order to be able to sense God, the Father-Mother-God, the love and the light, in us:

*I am the Order in God's All-Order.*

*I am the Order in God's All-Order,*
*which illuminates my disposition.*

*I am the Order in God's All-Order,*
*which shines throughout the content of my thoughts.*

*I am the Order in God's All-Order,*
*which makes manifest the content of my words.*

*I am the life in God's work of the deed,*
*in His creation, for people, nature and animals.*

*I am the Will in God's*
*Will of creation that brightens my disposition*
*and is the content of my thoughts.*

After going through the already given indications from the Primordial Light, it continues. But first, we might make ourselves aware that God's Will is a moving power that leads toward the deed. And so, His Will is the Will of creation, from which came the forms of Creation. We can say that God's Will is the "Let There Be."

And now, comes the next step, which addresses the Will of God in us, in our disposition, in our thoughts and in our senses. It says:

*I am the Will in His*
*Will of creation of the Let There Be.*
*Let there be more and more light in my awareness.*
*My five senses brighten.*

I repeat:

*I am the Will in His*
*Will of creation of the Let There Be.*
*Let there be more and more light in my awareness.*
*My five senses brighten.*

Let us allow this sentence that is given to us from the Absolute Law of God become effective in us, by once again thinking it slowly, consciously and intensely into us:

*I am the Will in His*
*Will of creation of the Let There Be.*
*Let there be more and more light in my awareness.*
*My five senses brighten.*

Once more:

*I am the Will in His*
*Will of creation of the Let There Be.*
*Let there be more and more light in my awareness.*
*My five senses brighten.*

The "Let There Be" will stir in the one who works with this consciousness aid day after day. Always, when difficult situations of the day or problem occurrences want to overwhelm us, deep from the very basis of our soul we sense the "Let There Be." And we can be sure that whoever entrusts himself to God in his inner being will also recognize the step that needs to be taken in the respective situation.

Dear brothers, dear sisters in Christ, let's not forget the seismograph, our invaluable admonisher, which always draws close to us when we give it the chance to be effective in us and through us. Let us open the door to our conscience to it. If we invite it to step in, in order to be effective in us, we will experience more and more our inputs, the blueprint, in the cells of our body. Then we will grow more sensitive and our senses more light-filled. However, the prerequisite for this is the application of what the Primordial Light speaks to us and which the seismograph announces to us.

From people who are becoming more light-filled, go out ever more light-filled thoughts, through which the Spirit of the Christ of God can shine and be effective.

We are on this earth, to dismantle our blueprint – the negative, human programs we have brought with us – in order to accept the creation thoughts that speak in our soul: "My child, let it happen – I will serve and help you. My child, come home after your sojourn on earth! I, your heavenly Father, want to have you again at My side. You and I want to see each other again, face to face. Know, my child, I love you and long for you. Join in, helping the "Let There Be" break through in ever more people, and the earth become more and more light-filled. Let your life, which I am, My light, shine over the earth, as a sign of My presence."

Dear brothers, dear sisters in Christ, I want to add nothing more to these heavenly words than to say: Let there be light in us and on this earth!

Linked in divine love,

*Gabriele*

*God's* Holy Will
Shines in My Senses,
Thoughts and Words.
The Cells of My Body
Are Renewed.
My Soul Brightens.

Will 3

# Will 3

$\mathscr{D}$ear brothers and sisters in Christ, in our time, during which all good customs and values melt away like snowflakes in the sun, it sounds like mockery to read the following words: "The peace of the heavens comes to the earth, the Kingdom of Peace, announced by the Eternal from the very beginning, as Fall beings began to emerge in human form."

The Kingdom of Peace is coming! This *is* the truth. It is coming because God – the Eternal, the life, the beauty, the purity, the love and the peace – is the immutable word. His word holds true for the earth and for all material forms and substances, for God is the life that is present in every atom, in all the forces of matter.

Let us become aware of the fact that God spoke at all times through God-filled men about the Kingdom of Peace, the Kingdom of God on earth. The records which mankind knows about – also concerning the Kingdom of Peace – are young in years compared to the revelation directed by the Eternal to the first human beings on the planet Earth: that the spiritual substance of the earth, which is in the animals, plants and minerals, is a part of the Kingdom of Eternity, just as are the spiritual substances in all dense-material stars and planets.

What is a part of the eternal Kingdom of God will also return to the eternal Kingdom of God. This fact led to the announcement of the Kingdom of Peace on earth which then followed, ever since – as measured over ages past – messengers of light commissioned by God for this task called this to mind in those who were emerging in human form.

Already at the beginning of the Fall-event, when rebellious spirit beings left the kingdom of light of the eternal heavens, it was clear that all spiritual substance, all pure forces and pure beings would again slip back into the formation of heavenly unity.

The word of God is the truth. The first humans accepted the word of God, the truth, just as little as has been done at all times. And during the present time, called the end-time, the announcement of the coming of the Kingdom of God, of the Kingdom of Peace of Jesus Christ, is also taken seriously just as little.

What does end-time mean? It means the end of the sinful age; the end of everything that was established on the earth by sinners, to the detriment and harm of Mother Earth with her animals, plants and minerals; it means the end of the sinful, human creature, that maltreated and still maltreats the earth, that exploited and still exploits God's creation, trampling it underfoot. It is written in the following sense: A new heaven and a new earth will emerge, which means that the old, the sinful state of things, will be dissolved.

How shall this take place?

A picture can convey this best: A seed that lies in the soil can sprout and become a small plant, yes, even growing into a mighty tree, only when the elemental forces of sun, water, earth and air cause the seed to sprout. If this weren't so, if the elemental forces were to give the seed no nourishment, then it would dry up and wither away.

It is very similar with the Kingdom of Peace of Jesus Christ that is coming to the earth. The seed is the fine-material, the divine, primordial substance of the earth; we also call it the earth-soul, or talk about a part that comes from the Kingdom of God. This part in the material earth is made fruitful by the Spirit of God, which is also active in those people who not only pray for the Kingdom of God, the Kingdom of Peace, but do on the earth what God wants. People in His Spirit will bring the divine nourishment to the coming Kingdom of Peace of Jesus Christ: They will bring peace to the animals, attentive care to the world of plants and minerals. Such people are aware of the unity of life and of peace as a part of the All-creation.

People who fulfill the law of love more and more, so that the divine unity is manifest among humans, animals, plants and stones – that is, the unity with the Mother Earth – will possess the earth. From the work of individual people for the Kingdom of Peace of Jesus Christ, develops a mold, a matrix, which is an essential component in the Christ-of-God atmosphere that is being drawn over and around the earth.

Ever more people all over the world, who are linked with the Christ of God, receive among other things, impulses from the radiation of the Christ-of-God atmosphere that lead them spiritually further and higher. Through this, some find their way closer to God in their inner being; others, who have already gone a ways spiritually, experience and know in their hearts that the building of the Kingdom of God on earth, the building of the Kingdom of Peace of Jesus Christ, has begun. Still others sense that the Christ of God is coming toward the earth, for the Spirit of Truth has taken His feet from the footstool of the earth and placed them on the earth, which means that Christ is announcing His coming.

The emerging Kingdom of Peace is like a small seed. Through people, Christ has begun to establish a small Kingdom of Peace that grows in size and light. At the same time, the atmospheric matrix of the emerging Kingdom of Peace is developing, which calls the attention of people striving toward God to the coming of the Christ of God. Just as everything begins in a small way in the Spirit – remember the seed – what successively grows on the earth is what links heaven to earth: the Kingdom of Peace of Jesus Christ.

The justice of God is His love and wisdom – the rescue for all those who let themselves be guided by Christ. This is why the great and mighty Spirit offers us people once again the way into the Father's house, the path within. Because time is accelerating and the hours are flying by, God, our Father, offers us the shortest way – a stretch of path for which it is worth making the effort, in order to find our way, in a very brief time, into the Kingdom of God, into the Kingdom of Peace, which is in the very basis of our soul.

If we follow this direct and shortest path with utmost discipline and effort, then Christ, our Redeemer and leader, can guide us. And then, in us and on the earth, we experience what is spiritually taking place, and also what is starting to develop in this world. And then we understand what the statement means that says, "I make all things new, a new heaven and a new earth."

God is love. His love is incomprehensible for us human beings. He loves all His children, whether they are for Him or against Him. Christ, the Good Shepherd, goes after every little sheep to rescue it. Untiringly, He fights for every soul and for every person. We can understand this with our heart, if we deeply pray the Lord's Prayer and read the messages which God, the Eternal, gave through the prophets of the Old Covenant and which the Christ of God again gives today, particularly during the last 30 years.

In these, His messages for our time, Christ very often speaks of the Kingdom of Peace of Jesus Christ. The all-encompassing truth goes out into the whole world, into many countries of this earth. So that many people may learn about what is happening on this small area of the earth, which is still like a small seed, the Christ of God asked the Original Christians to establish a divine transmitter with the name:

*New Jerusalem Broadcasting*
*for the Kingdom of Peace of Jesus Christ*

We can see and feel the infinite love of the eternal Father and of His Son, our Redeemer. With the Primordial Light, by addressing the Absolute Law, we hear over and over again: "May the one who wants to save himself, save himself, before this world passes away."

Everyone who does not seek out the Spirit of the Christ of God in the churches of stone, but strives to find Him in his heart, in the very basis of his soul, will understand bit by bit that the time is ripe, that the seed is sprouting – for the Kingdom of Peace of Jesus Christ.

Dear brothers, dear sisters in Christ, the phrase "May the one who wants to save himself, save himself, before this world passes away" means for many people to follow the direct, the shortest path with discipline and effort. Let us follow it at the hand of the Christ of God and read once again the addressings of the Primordial Light that have already been given, the instructions that shorten the path to God in us, so that we soon grow closer to God in the very basis of our soul! Then follows the further step of light on this shortest path to God before this world passes away.

Together, let us think the wonderful radiation of love and of life of the Primordial Light into our body and deep into our soul. Our soul particles and our body cells now receive the radiation of the Primordial Light.

*I am the Order in God's All-Order.*

*I am the Order in God's All-Order,*
*which illuminates my disposition.*

*I am the Order in God's All-Order,*
*which shines throughout the content of my thoughts.*

*I am the Order in God's All-Order,*
*which makes manifest the content of my words.*

*I am the life in God's work of the deed,*
*in His creation, for people, nature and animals.*

*I am the Will in God's*
*Will of creation that brightens my disposition*
*and is the content of my thoughts.*

Now, the next step in which the Let There Be, the Will of God, is fulfilled. It is:

*God's holy Will shines*
*in my senses, thoughts and words.*
*The cells of my body are renewed.*
*My soul brightens.*

I repeat:

*God's holy Will shines*
*in my senses, thoughts and words.*
*The cells of my body are renewed.*
*My soul brightens.*

Once again I want to repeat this wonderful, All-wise sentence:

*God's holy Will shines*
*in my senses, thoughts and words.*
*The cells of my body are renewed.*
*My soul brightens.*

This absolute, universal and cosmic radiation of Will from the Primordial Light can change our whole human nature, if we see our days on earth in the light of this short pathway to God, our Father, in Christ, our Redeemer, above all, when we apply the just given absolute cosmic radiation of Will – *God's holy Will shines in my senses, thoughts and words. The cells of my body are renewed. My soul brightens.*

This happens when we often think it into our body and into our soul during the day. At the same time, we pay attention to the seismograph that we are already familiar with, which shows us in which of our five senses our weaknesses are still romping about, but which also addresses our subconscious, where thought vagabonds and word games that serve our own self-aggrandizement are up to their tricks.

If we appreciate the help of our seismograph and are willing to learn, we will valiantly go to work on many a pool of all-too-human brooding in us, and many a still existing attitude of reproach. Even the usual clichés, like, "Oh, my goodness" or "Oh, God, oh, God," or "For God's sake" or "For heaven's sake," or "Oh, my God," are addressed by the seismograph because its efforts are geared toward our becoming alert in relation to our own behavior patterns and not squander or waste our life force.

The one who consistently follows this path into the Primordial Light that shines deep in our soul will very soon notice, yes, he will feel it on his body, that the cell tissues, the components of his body, are cleansing because his soul becomes more light-filled. We see that we become lighter and more buoyant, that our disposition becomes sunnier, our body movements more harmonious and – speaking to older people – we become more youthful. Even our facial expressions change; our features smooth out – we have become more free and dynamic. Why? Because God's All-radiation, the wonderful Primordial Light that is God, our Father, in Christ, our Redeemer, shines increasingly more brightly in our soul and in the cells of our body, through which we live more actively and consciously.

We perceive our surroundings better and more deeply; we feel that we are imbedded in the communicative life of unity, which the realms of nature show us, that is, reveal to us.

Dear brothers, dear sisters in Christ, can I wish you, or all of us, anything more than the dynamic, eternal, inner fountain of youth that is the Spirit of God, the Primordial Light, in us? He is the health, the inner joy, the love for God and for neighbor, and a lot, a lot of cosmic life!

Linked in the eternal love that is God,

*Gabriele*

*My Being Is Light
of His Light. My Senses
and the Content of My Feelings,
Sensations, Thoughts, Words and
Works Are Thoroughly Illuminated.
I Am Free and Cosmically Alive.*

*I Am Aware that I Am for God,
and God, the All-unity,
Is for Me. And so, I Am the
All-unity in God's
Power of Being.*

Wisdom 1

# Wisdom 1

Dear brothers, dear sisters in Christ, God, the Eternal One, is calling. Ever since the Fall of the divine beings from paradise, from the eternal Kingdom of God, the souls that inhabit the worlds of the beyond and the people that inhabit the earth are being called by God, the Eternal, to come to their senses and change their ways. Through God-filled beings and people, God, the Eternal, has taught at all times the way back into the Father's house, from which all beings came.

Long ago, some of the Fall-beings of fine-material substance enveloped themselves in the coarse-material body, called human being. Ever more souls incarnated in human bodies. Their efforts were geared toward thinking and acting ever more *against* the law of God, which is the love for God and neighbor, in order to distance themselves more and more from God and from all things divine, by becoming progressively condensed. This is why they deliberately opposed the call of God, their, our, Father. They wanted their own realm.

And even as the Fall-thought of wanting to be God condensed more and more, God was not silent. Again and again, He sent His messengers to explain to the souls and people, to give them an understanding of the law of love and to show them the way that leads back into their eternal homeland, from where they once went out.

The Fall-beings wrongly believed that they would be able to conquer God by systematically building the opposite to His holy law: sin.

But God is invincible. He *is*!

God *is* – from eternity and in eternity.

Even if a person follows self-willed pathways – God and His absolute, immutable law cannot, nevertheless, be impaired by this, for God *is* – the law of love eternally, unchangeable.

Ever since the beginning of the Fall, the call of God has been carried into the Fall-worlds, the call that sounds out: Turn back and change your ways! Enter your divine heritage! Follow the path of love for God and neighbor, and return to the Father's house!

Many fallen beings did not want to listen. A large part of mankind has proven to be incorrigible and stubborn. When the caring hand of God kept being spurned, mankind's level of vibration sank so low that the souls were at the point of degenerating. So, Christ, the Co-Regent of heaven, went into incarnation. As the Son of Man, Jesus lived, taught and worked on the earth. He brought the support for the souls, the Redeemer-spark, which, seen as a whole, is a part of His divine heritage.

The deed of love of the Son of God on the cross brought a stop to the Fall-event, for the Redeemer-spark hinders the dissolution of the soul bodies. Every burdened soul, even that of the darkest demon, bears in itself, through the cosmic gift of the Christ of God, the mighty Redeemer-light, the Redeemer-power. And so, every single soul will ultimately have to acknowledge – even if many do so only after eons of suffering – that:

God, His holy law, *is*.

Although during the more than 2000 years since Jesus of Nazareth, God's admonishers and proclaimers have come forward more and more to awaken in people the longing for the eternal homeland and to move them to orient their life to the true teachings of Jesus, it looks worse than ever on the earth today.

The sham-Christian churches, with their evil and unlawful machinations, saw to it that today's people know neither about the effects of the law of sowing and reaping, nor about the redeeming and liberating spark of light, the Redeemer-spark of the Son of God, Christ, that wants to shine for each one of us on our way into the Father's house.

This is why heaven once again bows with might toward the earth at the threshold to the New Era before the world passes away, in order to offer the divine truth and guidance on the way home, through the prophetic word. The Spirit of the Christ of God is now pouring from the horn of plenty of truth and of life during this time that is called the end-time for everything that has a low vibration. Christ makes true what He announced as Jesus of Nazareth: to send the Comforter, the Holy Spirit, which will guide the people into all truth. – This has been taking place for over 30 years now.

The word of God is given to us human beings in word and tone, in a never before existing wealth of divine instructions on how the individual – according to his state of consciousness – can start to take the pathway that brings him back into the Father's house.

The Christ of God taught and teaches again the way homeward, into the kingdom of light of heaven. He, the mighty, redeeming Spirit, gave and gives from the divine fullness – as much as can be expressed in the words of man, and as much as we human beings can understand, if we are of good will. During this time, the Inner Path is taught over and over again, being explained and interpreted anew, over and over again, so that every person who wants to can follow it, regardless of his momentary state of consciousness.

During the past years, the Spirit of God also explained in His word to the people about the law of sowing and reaping.

At the same time, He admonished them to carefully deal with the causes they had created, that is, not to intensify them, but to get rid of them little by little, so that the power of the Christ of God would be able to dissolve them. For it is only then that the redeeming light of the soul becomes a flame that shines on all cell tissues, all components of the body, so that things go well for the person, so that he is happy and becomes or remains healthy.

The great gift of the Christ of God that is incomprehensible for us human beings, the Redeemer-spark in every soul, is the liberating, helping and healing power, as well. In this way, the Christ of God is not only the Inner Physician and Helper, but also the Inner Physician and Healer.

Christ wants to help and support every person and every soul. His Redeemer-deed, His redeeming work, is to lead home in the love for God and neighbor.

So that we may understand under what prerequisites Christ, His Redeemer-light, can be effective in us, I want to convey to my brothers and sisters a picture that corresponds to our world on this side of life:

When we people feel sick, when we are plagued by pain or have a physical affliction or if by way of external influences we are caused a physical suffering or other, we go to a doctor. We describe our pain to him or explain to him what physically happened to us or what we had to suffer, for example, through an accident. The doctor tries to help us by suggesting a treatment or prescribing a corresponding medication. When we accept the suggestions of the doctor, but do not act accordingly, that is, if we do not undergo the treatment or take the prescribed medication, then the doctor will say: "How can I help you if you don't do what I have suggested?"

It is similar with the Inner Physician and Helper. Christ, the Inner Physician and Helper, advises us to use the energy of the day, to follow the indications that the day brings to every person according to those burdens or negativities that need to be cleared up by him on that day. For the planetary constellations radiate to the earth each day the energies of human evil deeds that are stored in them. From these, the individual receives impulses – in his feelings or thoughts or through disagreeable occurrences and events – that tell him what he can still pay off or perhaps even make amends for, with the help of the light of Christ in him.

The spiritual treatment is: Recognize yourself. Recognize yourself in the situations and events of the day, in everything that happens to you, and know that there are no coincidences, that nothing happens by chance.

Whatever you have entered into the stars does not come back to others, but solely to you, the programmer of the inputs, yourself.

And so, each day gives every person indications of how he can change his earthly existence for the good, if he is willing to recognize and change himself.

Over and over again, we hear about the law of correspondence that says: Whatever makes me upset, whatever makes me angry or whatever I negatively think about others corresponds to me; these are aspects of my own personal inputs, that are stored as negative energy formations and that come back to me at some point in time in the form of suffering, illness, need or other blows of fate.

The Spirit of the Christ of God admonished and admonishes us to recognize ourselves and to call on Him, the Christ of God, to ask Him for strength, for His support and for help.

He stands at our side, if we earnestly feel remorse for what we have caused to others, if we ask forgiveness of those we have harmed and also do our part in forgiving others. And if we no longer commit the same negative patterns of behavior, the redeeming light of the soul transforms the sins, that is, the shadows in our soul, into light and power. It is only then, as already indicated, that the light of the Christ of God, the helping and healing light, can radiate more intensely into the cell tissues, into the components of our body.

On this pathway of light, we receive help and healing. The Christ of God, the Inner Physician and Healer, thinks first of the benefit for the soul, because it is the soul that first attains the liberation, the light of God, before it is then radiated into the body.

So, if we remain in the consciousness of light of the Inner Physician and Healer, He can also direct many things in our body toward the positive. But if we merely *ask* Christ for support, help and healing and do not *do* anything that He advises – to orient ourselves to the commandments of God and to His teachings – then it is like the picture with the human doctor, when the patient affirms the treatment and medication, but does not apply it.

In other words, whoever merely asks, but does not use his days, that is, whoever may very well accept the spiritual indications but does not act accordingly, will hardly experience any divine help or healing. And then, the person remains in his shadowed existence. And why? He may affirm the light, but he does not let it flow into him.

Let us once again become aware of the fact that ever since the Fall-event, the Spirit of God has been calling to His children: Turn back and change your ways! The Christ of God has been doing the same for 2000 years.

Now, His call is more direct, that means, more clear and penetrating. Now, He is calling: May the one who wants to save himself, save himself, before this world passes away.

Until today, a large part of mankind has not understood that the Creator-God in Christ has now set out to go over the earth. He came 30 years ago in His word, to open for mankind the way into freedom. Now He comes to free the earth from the sins of man. The people have burdened Mother Earth with these, by having maltreated, and by still maltreating, Mother Earth, by having tormented, and by still tormenting, the animals, and by having murdered, and by still murdering, them. Through this, they have brought themselves into a condition where their cloak, with which they enveloped their soul, the human body, is becoming more and more porous. And the causes that were not cleared up – everything that the person tossed to the wind despite the admonishments and warnings from the Spirit of God – now come toward the offender.

The earth and all earthly forms of creation have been so tortured, mutilated and killed, that the time has come, in which the Creator-God in Christ, raises the earth, taking it up to Him.

This is the beginning of the coming Kingdom of Peace on the earth. The words of the Lord's Prayer are coming true – as everything comes true that has been announced by God, the light: His kingdom comes; His Will is done.

He also said: Let there be a new heaven and a new earth. The first signs have been set. The Christ of God prepares His coming.

For the earth and for human beings, this is an extremely great, incisive and far-reaching event of high cosmic significance. In ever faster successions, the effects fall in over the perpetrators, the harvest of what they have sown since the beginning of the Fall and, in a particularly crass way, during the last **2000** years.

Although scientists in our world are not aware of the great event taking place on the earth, they are announcing – from the spectrum of their understanding – unimaginable disasters. These, in turn, bring with themselves corresponding effects like illness, hardship and death to the people.

God is the love that gives and gives, that helps and saves – as long as the person grasps His hand. This is why the eternal Spirit – this time, God-Father *and* His Son, Christ – the mighty All-power, the Primordial power, extends His helping hand to us human beings once again. Perhaps, for the last time? We do not know! We should not speculate about this, but use the chance and take the admonishing call seriously: May the one who wants to save himself, save himself, before this world passes away!

The Primordial Light has already radiated the first steps of the quickest, the direct, way to the Kingdom of God, which pulsates in the very basis of every soul as light, power and the eternal homeland. So that we human beings may soon arrive, before this world passes away – that is, before the earth shakes off the pests, the troublemakers and all refuse – we want to make ourselves aware of the steps to the Kingdom of God in our soul over and over again.

I do not want to repeat each time here the wonderful indications and words of guidance to the Primordial

Light, to the light of the Absolute Law, in us. They are treasures of immeasurable value, which in their uniqueness, diversity and meaning, should be reflected upon by every individual for himself, in order to then be applied conscientiously, according to the corresponding degree of recognition.

Let us now turn to the last step that was given to us:

*God's holy Will shines in my senses,*
*thoughts and words.*
*The cells of my body are renewed.*
*My soul brightens.*

Today, the divine Will extends its hand to the divine Wisdom and reveals the next step that follows.

Let us think the words deeply into our body and into our soul:

*My being is light of His light.*
*My senses and the content of my feelings,*
*sensations, thoughts, words and works*
*are thoroughly illuminated.*
*I am free and cosmically alive. –*
*I am aware that I am for God,*
*and God, the All-unity, is for me.*
*And so, I am the All-unity*
*in God's power of being.*

I repeat what imprints our divine heritage:

*My being is light of His light.*
*My senses and the content of my feelings,*
*sensations, thoughts, words and works*
*are thoroughly illuminated.*
*I am free and cosmically alive. –*
*I am aware that I am for God,*
*and God, the All-unity, is for me.*
*And so, I am the All-unity*
*in God's power of being.*

Dear brothers, dear sisters, please do not forget that such wonderful, cosmic, universal steps can only build on the previous instructions for life. Let us heed what the radiation of the Primordial Light, God's Love and Wisdom, transmitted and transmits to us, and let us do His All-wise Will of creation, and then we will feel what this step of Wisdom means that I want to repeat once again.

We again think it into our body and into our soul, in order to hear from it the resonance for us:

*My being is light of His light.*
*My senses and the content of my feelings,*
*sensations, thoughts, words and works*
*are thoroughly illuminated.*
*I am free and cosmically alive. –*
*I am aware that I am for God,*
*and God, the All-unity, is for me.*
*And so, I am the All-unity*
*in God's power of being.*

This time, too, I want to indicate that the seismograph is always active and has its direct effect, provided that we take the steps toward the Primordial Light in our soul. The seismograph, our conscience, can become a good friend for us, if we allow it access to our still present shadow-realm, to all the not yet thoroughly illuminated soul particles and to our subconscious.

With the seismograph as our good friend that does not value-judge, but, without pressuring us, merely points out our life on earth to us; our days, which consist of our walk through life on earth, can be quite exceptionally interesting. If we want this, it sets into motion processes in our consciousness that very quickly let us become new people.

The light of our soul that shines more and more into the body also moves us, among other things, to look at ourselves more closely in the mirror. What do we come to realize? The reflection certainly shows us positive changes that can be traced back to the Primordial Light radiation, to the steps we are taking toward the Kingdom of God, that shines within, in our soul.

Dear brothers, dear sisters in Christ, the path to the Primordial Light is a one-of-a-kind path that is given to us so that we may come to recognize, among other things, the time in which this world finds itself.

God's love links. It unites all beings, souls and people. It is the cosmic life in the Mother Earth, on and over her. It links all those who strive toward God with all animals, plants and stones and with all the stars of the cosmos, for the Spirit of God is omnipresent.

United in the love for God and neighbor,

*Gabriele*

*In God's All-law,
in His Work of Creation
of Love and Wisdom, I Am
All-encompassingly Effective.*

Wisdom 2

# Wisdom 2

𝒟ear brothers, dear sisters in Christ, our Redeemer, many people are Original Christians in the Original Christian stream, which has never dried up over all the centuries. The Original Christian stream is the prophetic Spirit, the flowing life of unity, of love and of love for neighbor. The prophetic Original Christian stream starts from the primordial power, from God, our heavenly Father. He is the imperishable life in the soul of every person. Because God is the Father of all people and beings, we are also brothers and sisters among one another.

We all have *one* Father, the heavenly Father, who beheld our innermost being, the pure being, in His infinitely eternal light and created us according to His law of love. His eternal, holy law is the origin, in which the emerging spiritual-divine form, the spirit being, matured and grew. The spiritual steps of evolution, steps leading to the developing spirit being, I call the "spiritual cradle."

Our innermost being, the divine body in our soul, is compressed law of love, and thus, it is heir to infinity.

Every divine being consists of the spiritual particle structure in which all basic powers of the Being are active – the whole universal law from the divine Order all the way to Mercy; these are the natures and attributes of God. And so, our spirit body is spirit of His Spirit, light of His light, love of His love – in the image of our heavenly Father.

Let us refer back to the spiritual-divine cradle, in which the developing divine body receives the shape and form that is given to it. In the divine cradle – on the path of evolution through the divine spheres of development – a nature form very gradually develops, in which the basis for the perfect spiritual body is inherent. If the nature form has matured sufficiently, then, according to its spiritual radiation and mentality, it will be attracted by a divine dual couple of the same radiation intensity.

The matured form of being, the nature form, imbeds itself in the spiritual, divine radiation shell, also called cocoon, created by the dual pair. In this energetic radiation shell, the spiritual cocoon, the form of being then unfolds into a spirit being.

The shadowed form of spirit being that lives outside the pure Being – that is, in the Fall-realms – is called "soul." When it incarnates, it enters a coarse-material, that is, physical, body, while incarnating.

Our spirit body consists of spiritual particles. The physical body of a person, on the other hand, consists of cells. Through the human process of procreation, a cell structure develops in the woman, that is, in the womb, that grows and develops into a fetus. It is a shell of cells, into which a soul will incarnate.

When the human child, the baby, is born, then the soul within is always linked with the same or similar aptitudes and predispositions of the parents. For already at the point of procreation what holds true is: Like draws to like.

The approaching soul thus links up with these aspects in the soul of its parents. The like-vibrating magnetism of both parents attracts the soul prepared for incarnation, which links bit by bit with a cell body and becomes the child of the new parents. Either the parents and child have some debts from previous lives to clear up together, or they are linked through a spiritual commission for the Kingdom of God.

The newborn is laid in a little bed by the parents, which I, in turn, want to describe as a "cradle." First, the active radiation of the soul of the newborn shapes the body of the child.

During the course of the baby's further development, when the soul takes possession more and more of its physical body, the active energetic inputs that the child has brought along take effect on the prepared cell structure.

Whoever knows about reincarnation is aware that no energy is lost, neither the positive nor the negative. Through the content of his or her acting or not acting, every person erects a so-called matrix for the next incarnation of the soul. This matrix consists of corresponding energetic inputs and takes on form in the material cosmos. With the now imminent and new incarnation, a cell state, an army of cells, forms the body of the person according to this matrix.

Let us be aware of the fact that every cell of the body is a memory bank. Whatever the soul lets flow into its physical body brings about the beginnings of perception in the brain of the little human child.

Every cell, every component of our physical body registers right from the beginning the content of our feelings, sensations, thoughts, words and actions. And so, we can refer to the cell memory, whereby every cell structure has its specific cell memory.

The child, which still lies "in the cradle," and later when it begins to walk, is dependent on the parents. The basis upon which the child builds, the talents and predispositions that are also recorded in its cosmic matrix, were brought by the soul from its previous incarnations. Now, it is up to the parents how they will guide their child. If they are willing to question their own negative characteristics, for example, malice, quarrelsomeness or their lack of morals, in order to overcome them, they will also raise the child accordingly, responding to it in the same way.

At first, the child registers things with its sensory perception of sight, hearing, smelling, tasting and touching – that is, those things that are mostly determined by the influence of the parents. This is what they give the child for its continuing path through life. When later the five components of feeling, sensing, thinking, speaking and acting become active, these will become the tools for the child's actions. In this way, the young person becomes independent, because the five perceptions of seeing, hearing, smelling, tasting and touching flow into the five tools of action – of feeling, sensing, thinking, speaking and acting – and in this way, the person can discriminate between good and bad. He is independent and thus, also responsible for all that he does or does not do. Self-responsibility is decisive for his personal life on earth.

Whoever can affirm this course of life on earth from the cradle on, now also understands how important the commandments of God and the teachings of Jesus, the Christ, are, and that these should be the criteria used in the education of the child and are decisive for the continuing earthly life of the growing person. No matter what the soul has brought along with it for its existence on earth – the young person is later responsible for his own feeling, thinking, speaking and acting.

Let us be aware of the fact that every person registers and records from the cradle to the grave. The content of all our feeling, sensing, thinking, speaking and acting are first absorbed by our brain. Our brain then passes this on to the respective cell systems, either the cells of the liver or the stomach, or the lungs, etc., namely, always to those cell systems that correspond to the vibrations or frequencies of the impulses coming from the brain. There, they are then stored as energy.

Thus, every cell tissue, even every individual cell, yes, every component of our body, has a long-term memory that is in constant communication with the brain as well as with the inputs in our soul and, beyond that, with the corresponding repository planets, in which are also stored the energy potentials created by the person.

Whoever has not stopped learning, knows himself ever better, for the character of the individual person develops from the content and processes of the activities of his organs of perception and implementation. So how does a certain action come into being?

As soon as we see or hear or smell, taste or touch something that corresponds to our active inputs that have been registered, the perception begins: Our nervous system, the resonance board of our body, comes into a certain vibration. Pictures rise up. The components of implementation of feeling, sensing, thinking, speaking and acting come into action. Emotions move our mind. We begin to think. Perhaps we feel urged to express ourselves, to verbally "clear the air," or we may even want to act, for example, bringing our agitation, our inner tumult, into action. For the one who does not go passively through his days, the question is now raised: What is it that is moving me, making me upset?

Whoever has learned to take what preoccupies him or even wants to force him into a certain action and to lay it in the scales of the for or against – that is, to weigh it to see whether it is good, less good or even bad – is thus switching on his conscience, his "seismograph," in order to sound it out and perhaps even clear up the negativity. If, after this, he no longer does the same or similar thing, then he very gradually frees himself from what is not good, from what later in his life might have dealt him a raw deal or even negatively influenced his whole life on earth.

However, in our cell-state there is not only what is conditioned by the human that is active, but also the spirit consciousness – for some, more latent, for others, less. For this reason, the cell memory sends impulses to us from the source of life, from our true being – the positive! If we perceive it, we can move it in us. We begin to think. Now it is again up to us: Do we multiply the treasure of life, the good, which is a sliver from our all-encompassing divine heritage? Or do we heedlessly overlook the gift, not letting it unfold? Or do we reverse the message of the divine in us into its opposite, by aggrandizing our still present ego with it?

Everything, but everything, that we continue to spin via the five components is absorbed by the brain and passed on to the cells of our body. At the same time, the content goes into the soul and into the corresponding repository planets.

Let us take note: Even if the person deceives himself about the true value of his stirrings and actions – the brain as a controlling mechanism does not let itself be deceived. And the cell memory does not forget anything, neither the positive nor the negative. We can dissolve our negativity solely with Christ, our Redeemer, by surrendering it to Him. He transforms it – insofar as we are serious about changing our ways – into positive power. Through this, our soul radiates increased light, divine power, and our brain cells pass the light on to our body cells. To the extent that the cells of the body cleanse themselves and become more light-filled, the person becomes or remains healthy, or he avoids a blow of fate.

The cell memory, from which the negativity flows out and dissolves more and more, sends the light – the high power from God and the light of our Redeemer, Christ – to the corresponding sensory perception of seeing, hearing, smelling, tasting and touching. The result of this is that our five components of implementation – feeling, sensing, thinking, speaking and acting – are ennobled. This leads to the development of a finer character and to a God-conscious behavior in our whole life on earth, in our family, in partnership, with friends, at work and so on.

Whoever has read attentively now recognizes and understands why the Eternal, God, our Father, again gives us the path to the divine basic law, to the All-law, the levels of the law from Order to Will, to Wisdom, to divine Earnestness, to Patience, which is the same as kindness, to Love, to Mercy, which is the same as gentleness.

Why does God, our Father, address us on this in manifold ways over and over again? Because the All-law of love, the All-law of God, is our divine heritage. And if we people choose this as a standard for our life, our conscience will work all the more strongly. It is the seismograph, that supports and helps us to recognize what is against our divine heritage. These not good things can – based on the law of cause and effect – become our doom and then come toward us in the form of suffering, hardship, illness or another form of misfortune.

If we cherish the Primordial Light, our divine heritage, the steps which the Eternal, the infinitely eternal power, has already given to us and if we work with this day by day, then, in us, the divine source of life opens, which is the longing of our soul.

Let us accept thankfully the further step from our divine heritage, which the Primordial Light radiates to us and which conveys to us the Wisdom, the deed!

From God, our Father, the Primordial Power, which is our life, we receive the next step, and it is:

*In God's All-law,*
*in His work of creation of love and wisdom,*
*I am all-encompassingly effective.*

I repeat, and we allow these words of light – if we want to – to flow into our body cells, into the cell-memory:

*In God's All-law,*
*in His work of creation of love and wisdom,*
*I am all-encompassingly effective.*

I again repeat:

*In God's All-law,*
*in His work of creation of love and wisdom,*
*I am all-encompassingly effective.*

Let us seriously think about the absolute words of love and wisdom by examining our life situation and asking ourselves: Am I willing, do I even want to let go of my sinfulness, in order to accept and fulfill the word of God, which is absolutely spoken?

As long as we affirm and accept the word of the eternal life, we also say yes to our conscience, the seismograph, which, from time to time, knocks at our door ever more intensely.

Dear brothers, dear sisters, I ask you to take God's all-encompassing help, His all-encompassing helping hand, very seriously! Whoever treats it lightly by thinking the words into himself or speaking them into himself without taking the necessary steps for his thinking and for his life, nevertheless does set the seismograph into motion. Whoever does not heed the indications about the all-too-human aspects, that is, whoever does not repent of the wrong attitudes that the seismograph exposes, and thus clears them up with the help of the Christ of God, by no longer thinking, speaking and doing the same or like thing, will have difficulties in his life, which mostly begin with a certain restlessness and an instability in his thinking and doing.

But if, with Christ, the person puts order in his life on earth, he attains Wisdom, because his senses, the organs of perception are cleansed and the five components of implementation – feeling, sensing, thinking, speaking and acting – are brought into line with the senses that are cleansing. This results in an inner strength of resolution, in purity and stability. The person begins to ever more consistently weigh and measure what he sees and hears. And then he will be able to resist the temptations, the stimulations, offered by this world. This brings about strength of character and a meaningful life.

Dear brothers, dear sisters, only a true, meaningful life unites us with God, our Father, and makes us happy from within.

I wish you, I wish us all, the experience of the happiness of an alert soul and person.

*Gabriele*

*In My Divine Heritage*
*Is the Work of the Deed*
*of the Divine Love,*
*Wisdom and Justice.*
*God's Love, Wisdom and Justice*
*Are Fulfilled in My Thinking,*
*Speaking and Doing.*

Wisdom 3

# Wisdom 3

$\mathcal{D}$ear brothers, dear sisters in Christ, let us read what the law of God, which is love, wants to tell us.

The law of the Eternal is immutable, since it is absolute, that is, complete and perfect in itself. This is why it cannot be changed, not by any being, nor by any person.

Many know that the eternal law consists of the seven basic powers of Order, Will, Wisdom, Earnestness, Patience, the same as kindness, Love, and Mercy, the same as gentleness, and that every basic power is contained in the others as a sub-region. And so, there are seven-times-seven law-forces, which flow into one another and are like a crystal that reflects all facets of the eternal law.

From this volume and substance of the eternal law – the seven-times-seven divine powers – is also created the divine body, the spirit body of the heavenly being. This is the radiation of every heavenly being. And thus, the spirit being is a source of light-energy from God.

Because the divine body of the heavenly being is the eternal, holistic law that has taken on form, every divine being is an heir to infinity. Because of this, not only are all heavenly planes open to it, but they also belong to it as essence and power; they are its heritage. For this reason, in all of the eternal Being there is no competition, for there is no "mine and thine," no "for me" and "for you," since the Being belongs to each one, equally. With this, every divine being is equal to every other, and they are in absolute agreement, that is, they are as one. With their spiritual mentality, which is the same as their spiritual capabilities, they personify the heavens and are effective according to their nature. It is in this that also lies the lawful principle of unity, as well as the justice of God.

With its mentality, or, capability, which can also be described as its talent or talents, every heavenly being bears responsibility for the whole. This means that through its activity, which corresponds to its mentality, its capability, that is, its talents, the divine being gives from itself the energy for the benefit of infinity, for the benefit of the Kingdom of God, which, as stated, is, as essence and power, the heritage of every heavenly being. And so, every spirit being contributes to the further growth of the Kingdom of God, by creating and forming from its potential of light-energy. The work together, in responsibility for the Kingdom of God, is the true, divine common good, the good for all.

Most human beings are not aware of the fact that in the innermost recesses of our soul we are heirs to infinity – as it is with the spirit beings of the pure Being. The awareness of our divine origin, of our inner being, is covered over by all that is basely vibrating, for example, by the ties to matter, by egoistically human, wishful thinking, and other things.

This is why the human being is marked by egocentricity – the one more, the other less. The narrowness of the horizon of his spiritual awareness distorts the person's view of greater interrelationships, and of the suffering and illness of his neighbor and second neighbor, the animals; the person is not embedded in the unity. Claims to power and dominion, which, in the final analysis, are based on the lack of a sense of inner security, have inequality as a consequence. Many work, while others have work done for them. These are violations against the justice that is anchored in the divine law.

The actions of the divine beings are just, because all are equal heirs to the Being, to the law of God, the Love, the Wisdom and Justice. That is, they are active in the all-encompassing work of the deed of the Being, because they are integrated in their divine heritage – all equally equipped with the same gifts of life, the All-law that is absolute. Because this is so, they give and are active from themselves.

This means that they also receive energy from the Eternal in rhythmic cycles, in the course of the eons on the heavenly planes, and thus, they receive far more than they have given, that is, than what they have contributed to the Kingdom of God with their mentalities and capabilities or talents. As soon as the primordial power, the Spirit of God, flows more intensely into the plane of heaven that is closest to the Primordial Central Sun, it is also allotted increased energy, through which this heavenly region expands and, as a result, gains in light-energy, primordial power. The divine beings on this plane of the heavens also receive accordingly, the light and power, the Primordial Light.

The divine principle is absolute perpetual motion that is absolutely balanced and based on giving and receiving. This, too, is the justice of God: Whoever gives selflessly also receives.

Many a one who grasps this principle of life will sit up and take notice, and perhaps draw the following conclusion: If this is the way it is, then it must also be the same way in the temporal, because God is the Absolute Law in all things. – And this is how it is.

Now, we want to continue to weave these thoughts together. Since the law of God, the selfless giving and receiving, holds true in the material universe as well – what does this mean for mankind and for the individual? Whoever thinks more deeply about himself will question himself by using the spiritual knowledge that he has received from the Kingdom of God. For example: What have I given selflessly, without receiving thanks or expecting anything in return? Or, what may I have demanded in return? Have I increased my talents and put them to work for the Kingdom of God, or have I buried them? And if I have increased them – for whose benefit?

Let's now take a large leap in our thoughts and think of the prophets of the Old Testament and then think of Jesus, the Christ, who brought us redemption.

As we know, God is the absolute, giving law of love, wisdom and justice. At all times, God sent enlightened men and women and prophets, to reveal to the people of all epochs of time what their divine heritage is. Whoever took the word of God seriously, took steps toward the fulfillment of the words of God and followed up with deeds in order to create a better, God-pleasing world, also received the gifts of love and the help to increase his talents – for a world in which higher values bear fruit and for the benefit of the people striving toward God. Aside from this, God also gives His strength for health. God gives food, shelter and clothing, of course, everything within the framework of justice and unity, in the awareness of equality and brotherliness.

With the gifts of God, material wealth for the individual is not meant, but receiving from the life of God that measure of well-being that is due to him according to his state of energy. The principle of unity means: One for all and all for One, who is God. It is the principle of the heavens and of the divine beings.

Let us remember what Jesus brought to this world! He caused a part of His divine heritage to flow into all burdened souls, including the incarnated souls, the human beings. The mighty, redeeming power from the spiritual heritage of the Christ of God divided itself into sparks and implanted itself in all souls, as already written in detail in a number of Universal Life books.

After Jesus, the Christ, enlightened people came, over and over again, who wanted to bring to life the law of God, a life in unity and true brotherliness for their fellowman. People of all epochs of time have heard and taken, that is, they received, but have given very little. Many not only remained the old sinners, but shadowed themselves ever more, and did what they are still doing today – the exact opposite of what the enlightened people taught, that is, brought to them from God.

Jesus, the Christ, gave the greatest, namely, a part of His divine heritage. With this, He stopped the degeneration of the souls. He prevented their dissolution.

Thus, He turned away, for all time, the danger of the immeasurable torture of the dissolution of a soul. Instead of dissolution, since then it is redemption – through Jesus, the Christ.

The care of God for His children is immeasurable. For over 30 years, a great, all-encompassing gift to all His human children is flowing from God's love and wisdom. It is His message from heaven. Christ makes true what He promised as Jesus: to reveal the whole truth insofar as it can be given and understood with human words. At the same time, He announced His Kingdom of Peace on earth, which is showing itself already today as a small building block that increasingly gains form on the tortured and maltreated earth.

We continue our train of thought and draw a line to the humanity of all generations. What did the majority of people do with God's word, with His rich gifts of love and wisdom? In our time as well, most people may have taken the word from heaven, but more than a few of them have trampled it underfoot, that is to say, they have "buried their talents." Thus, the fact of the word of God was noted, but no conclusions were drawn from it. By far, the majority of people remained in the recruiting service of the churches, recruited through baptism and thus, tied into a system that is against the teaching of Jesus, the Christ, against the love, the unity, the freedom and brotherliness. And others strive for personal, earthly wealth, for profit and honor.

And another type of person wants to imitate those who have reached the top of the social ladder. The consequences of this spiritual desertion are the "mine and me," out of which grew and grows envy, resentment, hatred, and thus, divisiveness.

Instead of unity and brotherliness, more and more animosity developed and an increasing division of the earth into parcels and lots. From this developed war of brother against brother, fratricide. The destruction of nature led to the torture of animals, all the way to animal cannibalism. Human beings consume their second neighbor, the animals, who breathe the same air as we people, that is to say, they have the same breath that supplies them with the same life force that we also receive.

What has become of human beings? Generally speaking, they have become walking corpses with very little spiritual, divine values. The behavior of mankind in the past and today is driving the world to its tipping point, which can be described as a worldwide collapse. The apocalypse is looming: The bad seed of the one who deliberately turned away from God is sprouting. This harvest will befall the earth. The inextinguishable soul will take the burden that was inflicted on it by the person into the spheres of purification. We can say that the law of sowing and reaping is in full swing; the causal law is reaping a rich harvest.

God in Christ, our Redeemer, gave from the horn of plenty of life during the past 30 years. Most people did not draw a spiritual gain from this. Because it is the way it is, this world is no longer on the edge of the abyss, it is slipping more and more deeply into the grave of death, where many spiritually dead are up to their tricks. This is why, on the direct path of the Primordial Light given by God, it is said over and over again: May the one who wants to be saved, save himself, before this world passes away!

But many a brother or sister here and abroad could now object and say: "But I never heard of the speaking God until now; so I do not fall in the category of the masses of people who receive from the Eternal and yet do not develop the spiritual gifts, having buried them instead. So I could not bring any spiritual talents to contribute to the building of the Kingdom of God on earth."

How quickly we human beings explain things away, but this is merely an excuse, because who doesn't know about the Commandments of God, or the Christians about the teachings of Jesus, the Christ, about His Sermon and the Mount and His calls of woe? There are more than enough explanations and excuses. But the state of the earth sends out other signals. The suffering of the animals, the known and unknown illnesses of human beings, the countless wars on the planet earth, the worldwide so-called natural disasters show that the earth can no longer bear anymore and that gradually, what was inflicted on her by her tormentors will fall back on them.

God, the Eternal, gives and gives. Why? Because He loves His children. When we see the state of the earth and the fullness of the divine gifts, which, particularly during this time, the Eternal is giving from His full horn of life, then many a one asks the question: Is this unique and direct path to the heart of our eternal Father the last? Or is this primordial power that pours itself out a call, an awakening call? Is it a warning to mankind and, at the same time, a chance for all to get going and seize the divine anchor, which God, our heavenly Father, again lets slip into the hearts of the people, in order to save them from torment, illness, epidemics and hardship?

"May the one who wants to be saved, save himself, before this world passes away" is truly an awakening and warning call, also in view of the immeasurable spiritual gifts given to us by God! If they are unfolded by us, then the spiritual talents develop. Then the person contributes to building the Kingdom of God on earth and, at the same time, prepares the way for the spiritual return of Jesus, the Christ, so that His throne and that of the heavenly Father may come to the earth, and, with His light-filled steps, Jesus, the Christ, can walk through nature and the spiritually imbued places on the light-filled earth.

And so, from the seven divine basic forces, from the eternal law that is our divine heritage, the Eternal is trying to reach our inner being, the being that He beheld and created in the course of the seven-dimensional law. Happy the person that allows the Primordial Light to shine into his soul and into the cells of his body.

During this difficult time, which, from a material point of view, is becoming more and more hopeless because the earth is set for the harvest, God, our Father, is trying to bring us home, to lead us home into our innermost being, to our divine heritage.

The mighty Spirit again addresses an aspect of the basic power of Wisdom, our divine heritage. What today, tomorrow, that is, daily, wants to flow into our soul and into the cells of our body is the following:

*In my divine heritage,*
*is the work of the deed of divine love,*
*wisdom and justice.*
*God's love, wisdom and justice*
*are fulfilled in my thinking,*
*speaking and doing.*

I repeat the Primordial Light radiation, which we think into our inner being, into our soul and into the cells of our body:

*In my divine heritage,*
*is the work of the deed of divine love,*
*wisdom and justice.*
*God's love, wisdom and justice*
*are fulfilled in my thinking,*
*speaking and doing.*

I repeat:

*In my divine heritage,*
*is the work of the deed of divine love,*
*wisdom and justice.*
*God's love, wisdom and justice*
*are fulfilled in my thinking,*
*speaking and doing.*

We have hardly finished thinking or speaking the radiation of the Primordial Light into our soul and into the cells of our body and the companion we already know, the seismograph, makes itself felt by us. If we have accepted and received it in previous Primordial Light radiations, then we experience its work in our soul and in our subconscious. Its work begins by nudging out of the soul or out of the subconscious the opposite of the divine inputs, drawing it into the light of day, that is, into the conscious mind. From our conscience, rises a so-called "uneasy" feeling, a not-so-good feeling that induces us to clear up everything that is not good, practically wanting to drive us to do this. Either we accept the impulses and let them speak to us, or we suppress them. If we listen to our companion, the seismograph, which has become a good friend to many of us, and if we pay due attention to it, then it will reflect to us our unlawful aspects, either in pictures or as thoughts that it inputs into our subconscious.

The seismograph, which is our conscience, is effective according to our reactions. Either we are for it or against it – and it will behave accordingly. If we have taken the seismograph into our thinking and into our behavior, and if we work with it, then it will also point out to us our cell memory.

Let us pay attention to the following: If we have already become our all-too-human inputs because the unlawfulness that makes us un-free has become a habit, then the corresponding body cells have absorbed it and work against us, that is, against our own body. This means that it will then be somewhat more difficult to have positive information fed into the cell memory. Why? Because our inputs take a systematic course. At first, each one of us works with the five senses of perception of hearing, seeing, smelling, tasting and touching, and then with the five implementing components of feeling, sensing, thinking, speaking and doing.

And so, these are the sensitive tools of our body with which we work. At first, we feed our consciousness and then our subconscious. Via the subconscious it goes into the soul and into the repository planets. At the same time, we are programming the corresponding cells of our body. They hold onto what we input into them and then influence our body with it, for example, our lungs, our stomach, depending on the energetic vibration that comes from the brain as a signal, an impulse. This is the pathway on which negative programs develop into illnesses in the body, or into hardship and blows of fate.

And so, each one of us is the author of his own fate. But we can also be the one who clears up his own self-made causes in time.

And so, we can say that whatever lies in the different areas of cell tissues as vibration, can hit us as a corresponding fate, if we do not recognize and correct the cause in good time. This is why we should not dismiss what the seismograph, our conscience, reflects or says to us by thinking that there's enough time for what we have to do. Let us remember that we continuously record our inputs!

Dear brothers, dear sisters, again I would like to bring to life an aspect of our divine heritage given to us:

> *In my divine heritage,*
> *is the work of the deed of divine love,*
> *wisdom and justice.*
> *God's love, wisdom and justice*
> *are fulfilled in my thinking,*
> *speaking and doing.*

God, our Father, wants us to return to Him. Untiringly, He shines His Primordial Light to us, which is linked in us with the light of the Redeemer of the Christ of God.

Let us use this wonderful chance, before this world passes away!

Dear brothers, dear sisters, in spiritual loving care, a very warm, divine greeting:

Greetings in God!

*Gabriele*

*I Am the Earnestness in God's All-wise Four Natures. I Have Transferred the Reins of My Existence to God.*

*I Am His Divine Order. I Am His Divine Will. I Am His Divine Wisdom. I Am His Divine Earnestness.*

Earnestness

# Earnestness

*D*ear brothers, dear sisters in Christ, the Primordial Light radiation is the direct path of the law to the Kingdom of God, to our divine heritage, deep in the very basis of our soul.

From the divine Earnestness, the Primordial Light radiation admonishes us to continue expanding, conscientiously and earnestly, the previous Primordial Light radiations from the basic forces of Order, of Will and of Wisdom with persistence, to be able to thus take the steps toward the divine attributes of God, Patience – the same as kindness – Love and Mercy, the same as gentleness.

The earthly existence of the one who has applied and applies the Primordial Light radiation earnestly and conscientiously changes. Inner joy and thankfulness toward God grow, because his sensations, feelings, thoughts, words and actions become more light-filled, that is, closer to God. People who follow this path feel and sense the longing for the unfathomable divine ocean more and more, for the eternal homeland, the Kingdom of God in them.

For such people, symbolically spoken, the inner window of the soul opens, and very gradually reveals a view into a more light-filled being, through which the fragrance of the heavenly roses can flow into the disposition and into the thoughts. In such people, strength and joy in life rise, because the cells of their body are filled with the love for God. The longing for the attributes of the soul become tangible, for the kindness, love and gentleness. They are the attributes of the Father-Mother-God and of His children, the sons and daughters of God.

The Primordial Light radiation, the way to the Father-Mother-God is truly a gift of the heavens, particularly during this restless time, when the uncertainty and fear in the hearts of the people drive them into despair and hopelessness. We can hear and see ever more clearly that this world is heading toward the abyss.

Whoever gives up on himself, by not earnestly seeking answers to the questions about God and the beyond, will lose his hold on the rudder of his own personal life's vessel during this stormy time. Automatically, the question then rises: Who or what will seize the rudder of this person's existence?

This depends on what the person thinks, to where he orients his thoughts. An energy field, which is just like him and is interested in him, will then get hold of him and use him accordingly. It may even misuse him, among other things, by taking, that is, robbing, energies from him.

It is getting darker and darker in this world. Why? Because based on the causal law, a considerable abuse of energy causes mankind to weaken increasingly. How does this happen?

Life is communication. Communication consists of sending and receiving. On the earth, a person can send positivity as energy – and receive the positive back accordingly – as well as send negativity, what is not good. According to the causal law, the law of cause and effect, we then receive negativity back, that which is not good, because with whatever we exchange energy, that is what influences us and what we absorb. The law of cause and effect, of sowing and reaping, is based on this principle. It can also be described as the law of exchange and binding.

In our feelings, sensations, thoughts, words and with our actions, we send. A person binds himself to what he sends out that is unlawful, not good. Or he takes energy from those to whom he sends his negative energy, if they allow it. Because on the pathways of sending and receiving, energies are always flowing. Either the positive energies are flowing and intensifying – or the same takes place on a negative level. In a group of people, who are in agreement in an unlawful way of thinking and acting, the flow of negative energy is the result. Through this flow of energy, they are perhaps bound to a corresponding negative energy field that is only waiting in the atmosphere of the earth to enter into communication with the same kinds of forces.

How often haven't we heard from our fellowman: "I only want to do good. My thoughts and desires are in order." But is this really so? – Whoever has not learned to question himself does not know himself and is of the opinion that he is good.

What does "good" mean? – In the Spirit of God, the word "good" has a very deep meaning, because good is only God. He is the holy law of love that is good.

A divine being, a spirit being, would never say of itself, "I am good." Whoever thinks of himself in this way merely shows that he has to attribute to himself a certain quality of character that he, the human being, does not personify. The divine beings, on the other hand, live in the ocean, God, in the law of love. They do not need to confirm to themselves that they are good. The good, the life that is God, flows through and permeates them; it is their life's substance.

During this time, the power of light of God, the Primordial Light, flows mightily into the condensed spheres of the Fall. We are in the midst of a very special time of grace.

The willing person feels that God wants to direct him onto the steps that lead to the law of love that is good. The Eternal, who is the infinitely eternal law of love, the Primordial Light, calls on His children once again, to draw closer to Him before this world passes away.

The one who strives to take the steps that the Primordial Light has shown and is showing him, which is the way into the Kingdom of God that is within, in every soul – these are the steps of Order, Will and of Wisdom – this person has become alert and understands the earnestness that brings to the pilgrim journeying into the Kingdom of God, steadfastness, security and a feeling of being home, that is, the nearness to God.

These subtle inner perceptions, which characterize the awakening of the soul, let one feel what unity and togetherness with God-Father and Christ and with all brothers and sisters in the Kingdom of God is, but also the togetherness with the innermost part of the soul of every person. People who see kindness, love and gentleness through the opened window of their consciousness experience the priceless world of nature. They sense the subtle stirrings of the animals, plants and minerals. Mother Earth has then become mother and father to them.

God, the Spirit of truth, is always the giving principle, who richly gives to His human children via the earth. This deep perception is truly the fragrance of the heavenly rose, the love, with which the Eternal envelops His children and signals to them that the three attributes of filiation are the ocean of life.

Dear brothers, dear sisters, the best and most fruitful recognition is self-recognition. Let us honestly question our thinking and our life! Let us ask ourselves whether we have really taken the steps toward the ocean of life, toward the garden of God, from where the fragrance of the roses of love streams, that wants to permeate our soul.

However, the window of the soul opens only when we live the four natures of God to such an extent in our earthly existence that we can truly say: We have become better people – people who drew or are drawing closer to the love for God and neighbor.

Many people who have heard or read about the law of love for God and neighbor are of the opinion that they more or less personify the love for God. They think that in their thinking and living they bring character-istics of divine love to expression.

But it is wrong to think that it would be a sign of love to flatter one's neighbor or to let him do what he wants at his convenience, or even be of good will toward his all-too-human inclinations, thus fortifying these in him.

Note well: The free will of our neighbor, which is anchored in tolerance, should always be kept. Each one is free to do or not do what he wants, as it corresponds to his thinking and wanting. But tolerance is not appropriate when people violate the Order of God, His Will and His intelligence, the divine Wisdom. Here, we are called to explain in general terms – above all, when others are included in the calculations of human arbitrariness.

On a personal level, we do not have to tolerate what others want to force onto us. We can, we actually should, represent what we think, whether this corresponds to the law of God or not is another issue. The love for God and neighbor, which is the All-law, the life, can be applied only if the person who speaks about it has developed for the most part, the first four basic forces of Order, Will, Wisdom and Earnestness. Anything else is a sugar-coated form of love, with which many – particularly those who have a lot of spiritual knowledge – show off and condemn others who, according to them, have no love. Such statements are presumptions which show the wise one what spirit is before him. Because whoever condemns, rejects. And so, tolerance is just as much a balancing act as being of good will, of flattering or even using the word "love," when others are pilloried with it.

Let's take the words "love for God and neighbor" and shine a light on them: Whoever does not love God with all his heart and from the very depths of his soul cannot love his neighbor either. This statement, accepted as a lawful principle of freedom, could lead to self-recognition, which shows the person what he may still be lacking. But whoever *experiences* the love for God and neighbor in himself because he has taken the steps via the four natures of God, for him the window of consciousness will open, through which streams the fragrance of the heavenly rose into the person's world of the senses and perception.

God, the Eternal, in His work of creation of Order, breathes through Order, into His Will, through Order and Will, into His Wisdom, and through the three natures into the fourth nature, the divine Earnestness. The four basic forces form the basis for the attributes of filiation.

Via the four natures of God – Order, Will, Wisdom and Earnestness – the Almighty created His children according to His fatherly primordial heart, and breathed into them kindness, love and gentleness. And so, at first they received the composition of creation, that is, the structure of implementation, His four divine natures, and then, the breath of filiation of kindness, love and gentleness. In every basic power of God all others are always contained as sub-regions, so to speak. This is the holistic law that says: Everything is in all things, and all things are in everything.

And so, the love for God and love for neighbor can be opened up only via the four natures, which are the forces of creation and of implementation, the activities in the divine being. This is also true for the human beings who only too willingly try to use love and love for neighbor as a criteria and requirement for others.

In the Primordial Light, which is the Almighty, God's love for His children is effective. And so, the Primordial Light addresses His human children.

With the previous Primordial Light radiations, we experienced the way of the love for God and love for neighbor, which, as mentioned, began with Order. So that we understand the way to our perfection, the law of love, that is our divine heritage, and have a just measure for ourselves, we read once again the words of the Primordial Light of the three natures already given. Afterward, we turn to the fourth nature, of Earnestness.

The words of the Primordial Light radiations are:

*I am the Order in God's All-Order.*

*I am the Order in God's All-Order,*
*which illuminates my disposition.*

*I am the Order in God's All-Order,*
*which shines throughout the content of my thoughts.*

*I am the Order in God's All-Order,*
*which makes manifest the content of my words.*

*I am the life in God's work of the deed,*
*in His creation, for people, nature and animals.*

I am the Will in God's Will of creation,
which brightens my disposition
and is the content of my thoughts.

I am the Will in His Will of creation
of the Let There Be. Let there be
more and more light in my awareness.
My five senses brighten.

God's holy Will shines
in my senses, thoughts and words.
The cells of my body are renewed.
My soul brightens.

My being is light of His light.
My senses and the content of my feelings,
sensations, thoughts, words and works
are thoroughly illuminated.
I am free and cosmically alive. –
I am aware that I am for God,
and God, the All-unity, is for me.
And so, I am the All-unity in God's power of being.

In God's All-law,
in His work of creation of love and wisdom,
I am all-encompassingly effective.

In my divine heritage is the work of the deed
of divine love, wisdom and justice.
In my thinking, speaking and doing,
God's love, wisdom and justice are fulfilled.

Now, we address Earnestness, the fourth nature of God, which, like all others, wants to become active in us as our divine heritage.

We affirm the three previous natures through the words of the heart:

*Lord and Father,*
*seriously and conscientiously,*
*I fulfill the three natures for the most part,*
*to now practice in the fourth nature.*

Now we think very consciously and intensely into the very basis of our soul:

*I am the Earnestness*
*in God's all-wise four natures.*
*I have transferred the reins*
*of my existence to God.*
*I am His divine Order.*
*I am His divine Will.*
*I am His divine Wisdom.*
*I am His divine Earnestness.*

Again, we let these words flow deeply into our inner being:

*I am the Earnestness*
*in God's all-wise four natures.*
*I have transferred the reins*
*of my existence to God.*

*I am His divine Order.*
*I am His divine Will.*
*I am His divine Wisdom.*
*I am His divine Earnestness.*

These absolute statements, of course, activate the seismograph. It is truly a good planner that heeds each person's day, which is known to be the special day of each individual. What the seismograph conveys to us in relation to our absolute statements is brought unerringly into our consciousness within the context of the aspects of our day. We can recognize in the beating of our heart, or in the rhythm of our breathing, or via our solar plexus, what it wants to tell us via our conscience each time.

Our life on earth brings forth fruit only when we experience that the inner window opens and the fragrance of the heavenly roses blows gently toward us. It is only then that we begin to live, for God alone, is the life.

Dear brothers and sisters, let us once more speak the words of the Primordial Light into us. They want to awaken, move and strengthen our inner awareness:

*I am the Earnestness*
*in God's all-wise four natures.*
*I have transferred the reins*
*of my existence to God.*
*I am His divine Order.*
*I am His divine Will.*
*I am His divine Wisdom.*
*I am His divine Earnestness.*

Dear brothers, dear sisters, from the very depths of my heart I wish you, I wish us all, the heavenly fragrance of roses. It opens for us what true love is, what true joy, yes, what inner happiness and security is in Him, God, our Father.

The roses of the heart link us.
In inner fellowship,

*Gabriele*

*Now, I Take the Hand of My Loving Father, of My Faithfully Caring Redeemer, Christ, and I Do Not Let Go of It Anymore.*

Filiation

# Filiation

Dear brothers, dear sisters in Christ! Again, in this Primordial Light radiation, we can sense what it means when the Rose Gate opens.

Let us use this hour to first of all become aware of the fact that our soul is not of this world!

It is to be hoped for and desired, that ever more people come to understand that they may very well be human beings on the planet earth at this time, but that in the end, they do not belong to the earth.

The irrevocable proof for this fact is given in the demise of our physical body at the end of our earthly journey. At some point in time, death comes, whether we welcome it or not. This fact alone tells us that we are only guests on this earth.

The soul can take no possessions or property from this earth. Only those unlawful things it has done to its neighbor – and to the Mother Earth with her animals, plants and minerals – are what it carries with it in the garments of its soul, as it changes over into the beyond.

Many people still direct all their efforts toward prestige, wealth and a high standard of living. For the majority of people, that is the meaning and purpose of their life. Higher values, that would give the human race a higher worth are disappearing more and more. Each one has more or less become his own best friend.

Even religiosity, marked by church patterns of thought, causes hardly a ripple in the awareness and attitude toward life today. The attachment to empty, external forms – for example, liturgical forms – and the generally externalized approach to everything has led to indifference toward the spiritual, toward the inner life. Year after year, the same verse! And then the sermon, which often has become filled with clichés and is an absurdity to many a listener, who doesn't know what to do with it. His conclusion – often denied – it's all hot air!

The hot air expressed by the church has advanced to such an extent, that even the words "Christ" or "God," the all-encompassing Spirit, mean nothing to many.

Unfortunately, the viewpoint that says Christ and God are the same as the ecclesiastical institutions is still very widespread.

But the sham-Christian message is like an oracle that no one can interpret, to the point that no one even bothers anymore to ask: Who is God? Where and how can I find God? – And why? Many a one thinks: "Well, for this, we have the priests, the ministers and theologians who have studied God and, in the end, must know about Him. They will tell me what God wants. And I will do – more or less – what the priests say. That will surely be right."

But Jesus, the Christ, spoke in the following way: *"Truly I tell you, unless you change and become like children, you will never enter the kingdom of heaven."* He did not say: "If you don't listen to the Rabbi – the priests, the minister, the pastor – you will not enter the kingdom of heaven."

Anyone who does not have an analytical mind will have difficulty weighing matters impartially. But many a one who has looked more closely into church history asks himself whether theologians know anything at all about God or whether it is at all possible to even study God. In this way, many draw the conclusion that if we are supposed to be able to study God, then Jesus would have had to be a theologian, that is, a Rabbi. But Jesus did not speak up for theology. He also was no Rabbi, quite the contrary, because He spoke according to the following: *"But you are not to be called Rabbi, for you have one teacher, and you are all brethren."*

As a matter of fact, quite unusually clear words spoken by Jesus against the Pharisees and scribes have been passed on, whom He described as "blind guides," "hypocrites," "a nest of vipers" and "blind fools." Jesus stood up against theology, against the priesthood, or ministers and pastors.

Jesus wanted all people to be treated as equals. He was against "intermediaries" who place themselves between God and His child.

Whoever has learned to think more deeply will come to the conclusion that God would not have given us human beings the Ten Commandments through Moses and the teaching of love for God and neighbor through Jesus, if theology were the answer to it all. If church regulations and doctrines were supposed to have been the instructions for life that God wanted for us human beings, Jesus would not have brought us His wonderful and simple teachings in the Sermon on the Mount – the teaching that is given for a higher ethics and morals, and that brings about a better world.

The eternal Spirit, God, shows us in His instructions, in His message, the way back into the Father's house. It is the way that enables the soul to journey homeward after the passing of its physical body. And to where? To the Kingdom of God, into the eternal homeland, from which it once went out as a divine being.

The proof that God and His Son Jesus, the Christ, do not endorse theological studies, the study of God, is also found, among other things, in the prophets of God. They were neither ministers nor priests. They belonged to no caste of priests, to no elite group within human society that took on a special, lofty status. The true prophets of God came from the people and had to lead a life in the Spirit of God, in order to be able to receive the almighty Spirit, which then spoke to the people through them.

The Eternal One does not let Himself be locked into a church or a traditional liturgy – not even when ministers or priests wear liturgical robes, allegedly in honor of Him.

Jesus of Nazareth did not adorn Himself with gold-embossed robes to demonstrate a "dignity worthy of honor." This is the "tradition" of the churches, borrowed from paganism. God wants us to adorn ourselves, that is, to enrobe ourselves, with the virtue of love for God and neighbor. God is the omnipresent, flowing Spirit – not tradition. This is why the Eternal cannot be found in traditional, sacramental forms, and it is written accordingly: God does not dwell in churches built by human hands.

Ever more people can sense this and they are asking: Is there a God? Where is God? Who is God?

God is the living wellspring of eternal life in each one of us. He is in our soul and in every cell of our body, which He respirates with His breath. His breath is life. When the physical body passes on, the soul takes the breath of God – we say, our breathing, the life – into itself .

Every person can observe that with the birth of a child, the newborn breathes in with its first cry. With this, the soul is saying, "I have now arrived in my earthly body."

When the physical body passes on, the soul breathes its physical shell, the material body, away from itself, so to speak. By exhaling its last breath, the soul gives a signal telling the people around it that it has taken the breath, the life, to itself. With this, the human shell has its demise.

In view of the course of the coming and going of the soul, we become aware of the fact that the earth is only a way station for the soul. Each one of us belongs, far more, to the eternal kingdom, the city of God-Father, in which kindness, love and gentleness are the source of the eternal Creator and creating power, the immutable law of the heavens.

In every human body, deep in the very basis of the soul, is its divine being, that was beheld and created by God, our Father, the child, the son, the daughter, of the Eternal.

The Spirit of eternity breathed into the developing divine being its divine heritage, the law of the heavens, the eternal life. This spiritual core of our innermost being that lies in the very bottom of our soul is immortal.

So that our soul can return to the eternal life, to the law of love of the heavens, we human beings should live according to the law of the heavens, and, at that, in our feeling, sensing, thinking, speaking and doing. A part of this is also having trust in God, our Father, and in Christ, our Redeemer. Whoever entrusts himself to God also believes in the All-power and guidance of God.

As already mentioned, it is written: *"Truly I tell you, unless you change and become like children, you will never enter the kingdom of heaven."* What does this mean for us? Children walk at the hands of their mother and father. They entrust themselves to their parents.

Do we truly believe in God and do we affirm Him as the almighty Spirit of love? Then we should follow the commandments of God and the teachings of Jesus, the Christ, step by step. Every one, who believes in the existence of God should actually ask himself, in self-examination, whether he truly is willing to do God's will and to go toward the eternal Father at the hand of the Christ of God, in order to enter the Father's house as a child, as the son or daughter of God, without taking long detours.

The one who earnestly strives for this very quickly realizes that without order in his thinking and behavior, he will leave, over and over again, the path that leads into eternity, into the Father's house. And so, we are called upon to put order in our life, not only in our living space, but also in our feelings, sensations, thoughts, yes, in all aspects of our behavior.

I ask you to follow my words deep in your inner being!

Whoever puts order into his life gains a lot. He becomes more calm and collected. From this, develops the next step: the Will of God. What is the Will of God? This question already has in it the deed, for whoever wants to fulfill the Will of God keeps the commandments of God and the teachings of Jesus, the Christ.

The one who consistently orients himself to this orients his life to God and to His law principles. Through this, the person becomes ever more sensitive, that is, more permeable for the truth, for the law of kindness, love and gentleness. This means that he increasingly receives from the wellspring of God's grace and plans his days wisely, in order to gradually draw from God's eternal wellspring of love, as the son or daughter of God.

The spiritual tasks that he gives himself to fulfill lend him wings of Earnestness.

This is characterized by self-possession, alertness, justice, caring, and not lastly, the experience of creative unity. This person recognizes deep in his heart that everything forms a unit and no being is shut out from the ocean of life.

God's love, which is the ocean of life, encompasses all Being, the beings in God, the animals, the plants. The whole of the pure All-universe is the ocean and the primordial wellspring, all in one.

Heaven's window is open for the one who has taken the steps to the kingdom of the innermost being at the hand of the Christ of God and he has become the rose himself, one who loves God. He wants no more than to be the child of God, his eternal Father, to be His son, His daughter.

We can now understand why the Eternal conveys the sovereign law to us from His primordial wellspring, the divine Order, His Will, His Wisdom and His Earnestness.

The one who has devoted his earthly existence to the eternal primordial wellspring, the Creator-power of God, has become an ethically and morally high-standing person. His feelings, sensations, thoughts, words and actions contain more and more selflessness, the justice that is anchored in the four creation-forces of Order, Will, Wisdom and Earnestness.

In the last Primordial Light radiation, we read about the inner window of the soul that very gradually reveals the view into a more light-filled being, through which the fragrance of heavenly roses flows. The heavenly roses symbolize the love for God and neighbor. The love for neighbor cannot be fulfilled without love for God, because God is the primordial wellspring of love, which, with His light, vivifies God's love for neighbor.

Let us again remember the words of Jesus: *"Truly I tell you, unless you change and become like children, you will never enter the kingdom of heaven."* Whoever takes a closer look at this statement recognizes, among other things, that without humility, reverence and respect before God, our eternal Father, there can be no unity between human beings, animals and nature, no unity with pure infinity.

The garments of our soul lie like thick veils over the truth, over the love and unity, over our divine heritage. The one who has not worked out the high consciousness of the All-unity that was made possible for us through the redeeming and liberating power of Christ has not thoroughly illuminated his soul garments. This means that despite spiritual knowledge, he has not drawn closer to the primordial wellspring of life.

But whoever worked with the Primordial Light radiation as the Eternal explained it to us has experienced not only a tangible, but also a visible, transformation. His disposition is lighter and brighter; his inner being is more steadfast; fears have disappeared. Worries are questioned and are put in order with the help of the Christ of God and, if possible, resolved to such an extent that the disposition brightens again, since the trust in God and Christ has remained steadfast, stable.

The growing trust in God and His guidance reminds many a one of the formulation of the previous Primordial Light radiation: "I have transferred the reins of my existence to God." For the individual, this could mean, for example: "Now, I take the hand of my loving Father, of my faithfully caring Redeemer, Christ, and do not let go of it anymore."

For people in the Spirit of love, the word "loving," which many use inappropriately, has changed into love for the soul in neighbor.

The person who is oriented to God no longer feigns love. He is good to the other one from soul to soul, without using any flattering words. His deeds are often works for the Kingdom of God, which he senses and feels in his heart, and with which he is linked. His prayers are filled by the love for God, his Father, and his works are prayers to the Creator, who loves His creation.

The prayers to God, who is the love, gradually encompass the whole of Creation-Being. People in the Spirit of God, in the love for God and neighbor, immerse more and more into the ocean of love, into the divine, all-eternal law of love. They have arrived home in the Kingdom of God, in their innermost being. The window of the soul has become the gateway to heaven, through which the loving ones of the homeland come toward the new arrival with roses of love, to go with him very soon through the inner rose gate.

Dear brothers, dear sisters, if it is this way with the one striving toward God, then the seismograph has done its job. The person who approaches the gate to heaven no longer needs any consciousness aids – he has become the light of the Father, the son or the daughter of God: a being of infinity. He is home, eternally.

Dear brothers, dear sisters, a preview and a small, humble insight for all those who truly applied and apply the Primordial Light radiation, who have an inkling of what the true love for God and neighbor means.

I wish you, all of us, the opened heavenly rose gate. God, our Father, longingly awaits us, His children.

Let us allow ourselves to be guided by Christ, our Redeemer, brother and friend.

Linked in the love for God and neighbor,

*Gabriele*

# Appendix

# Books in the Universal Life Series

## This Is My Word –
## A and Ω – The Gospel of Jesus
### The Christ Revelation,
#### which true Christians the world over have come to know

A book that lets you really get to know about Jesus, the Christ, about the truth of his activity and life as Jesus of Nazareth.

From the contents: The falsification of the teachings of Jesus of Nazareth during the past 2000 years - Jesus loved the animals and always spoke up for them - Meaning and purpose of a life on earth - Jesus taught about marriage - God is not a wrathful God - The teaching of "eternal damnation" is a mockery of God - Life after death - Equality between men and women - The coming times and the future of mankind, and much more!

1078 pages / Order No. S 007en, ISBN: 978-1-890841-17-1

## The Message from the All – Vol. 1
### The Prophecy of God Today – Not the Word of the Bible

God does not forsake humankind, His children. For over 30 years now, He again speaks His direct word through His prophetess and gives answers to basic questions. From the great treasure of these divine revelations that were given in countless revelations, 14 have been selected and are now published for the first time.

187 pages / Order No. S 137en, ISBN: 978-1-890841-36-2

## The Word of the Christ of God
### to Mankind Before this World Passes Away
### Nearer to God In You

Believe, trust, hope and endure! What do these mean and how can we apply them on our way to God? How do we turn belief into an active faith? How do we develop trust? Hope is expressed in setting goals that are carried out with confidence. What does it mean to endure in the divine sense? Experience the Inner Path in condensed form. Simple clear words, given to all people who long for God and a fulfilled, happy life in freedom.

112 pages / Order No. S 139en, ISBN: 978-1-890841-45-4

## The Path to Cosmic Consciousness –
## Happiness, Freedom and Peace

The path to cosmic consciousness is the path to inner happiness and inner peace, to the feeling of having "arrived." Where? In the Kingdom of God, of which Jesus, the Christ, already taught that it can be found within, in every person. It is our true, divine being. This is a path of liberation, which Gabriele, the prophetess and messenger of God, walked ahead of us. As a guide, she showed how we can learn not only to fulfill our work more quickly and conscientiously, but also how we can make peace with our fellowman and with nature and the animals, and how we can maintain it. Through this, we become happy and free!

75 pages / Order No. S 341en, ISBN: 978-1-890841-60-7

## The Sermon on the Mount –
## Life in Accordance With the Law of God

Timeless instructions for a peaceful and fulfilled life. A path that leads the way out of the dead-end in which so many people find themselves today. An excerpt from a work of revelation "This Is My Word."

112 pages / Order No. S 008en, ISBN: 978-1-890841-42-3

## Live the Moment –
## and You Will See and Recognize Yourself

Now, in this instant, the state of our soul shows itself. We can see it in the feelings, thoughts, words and actions taking place at every moment in us. Become sensitive to what the signals of your inner life are telling you.

76 pages / Order No. S 315en, ISBN: 978-1-890841-54-6

## Where Did I Come From? Where Am I Going?

The wherefrom and whereto of our life is no longer a mystery. Following explanations on the important questions on life after death, answers are given to the 75 most frequently asked questions on this topic.

75 pages / Order No. S 315en, ISBN: 978-1-890841-09-6

## God Heals

There is a mighty, indescribable power in us. It is the central power of love, God's power and healing. Learn how to unfold this power!

61 pages / Order No. S 309en, ISBN: 978-1-890841-23-2

## Cause and Development of All Illness
## What a person sows, he will reap

A book more relevant than ever before, more exciting than a thriller, more moving than a docu ... Much revealed over 20 years ago by the Spirit of God is confirmed today by science: Without a balanced relationship between people, animals, plants and minerals, mankind will not survive in the long run. What will the future bring? What are the effects of man's destructive behavior toward nature, the animals and, not least, his own state of health? Learn about formerly unknown correlations and frontier zones between spirit and matter, about the effect of the power of thoughts, e.g., how harmful parasites and pathogens can be created by our behavior patterns, about holistic healing, the meaning of life on earth, and much more ...

360 pages / Order No. S 117en, ISBN: 978-1-890841-37-9

## You, the Animal – You, the Human Being...

An unusual book on animals that explains the emergence of the life forms of nature and the all-encompassing, effective and fundamental spiritual principles governing all of life. We learn about the communication between animals and nature beings, the possibility for people to communicate with animals, why animals attack us, the right way of treating them, and much more.

108 pages / Order No. S 133en, ISBN: 978-1-890841-25-6

## The Animal-Friendly Cookbook

Over the course of a lifetime, a person can save the lives of 450 animals, simply by not eating meat. This alone gives good reason to become vegetarian, or vegan! The bonus? You remain healthy and fit! This book is meant to serve all who want to contribute less and less to our world's environmental problems, to suffering in slaughterhouses and the inhumane conditions in factory farming.

208 pages / High-gloss color illustr. / Order No. S 436en
ISBN: 978-1-890841-57-7

*To order any of these books or to obtain a complete catalog of all our books, please contact:*

*THE WORD*
*P. O. Box 5643*
*97006 Wuerzburg*
*GERMANY*

*or:*
*Universal Life, the Inner Religion*
*P. O. Box 3549*
*Woodbridge, CT 06525*
*U S A*
*1-800-846-2691*

*or:*
*Universal Life, the Inner Religion*
*P. O. Box 55133*
*1800 Shepherd Ave., East*
*Toronto, ON  M2J 5A0*
*CANADA*
*1-800-806-9997*

*www.universal-spirit.org*
*e-mail: info@universelles-leben.org*

*or:*
*Order our books at Amazon.com*